Gratitude Journal

365 Daily Reflection Prompts

Sarah Melland

Copyright © 2018 Sarah Melland and Deb Bailey
Published by Ripe Melland Media

All rights reserved. No part of this publication may be reproduced, stored in a retrieval system, or transmitted, in any form or by any means, electronic, mechanical, photocopying, recording, or otherwise, without the prior written permission of the publisher.

ISBN: 978-1-7346333-1-3

Front Cover Design by: Sara Mason
www.saramason.wordpress.com

CONTENTS

Introduction	1
Law of the Ego	3
Law of Manifestation	19
Law of the Present Moment	35
Law of Free Will	51
Law of Relativity	67
Law of Resistance, Attachment, and Detachment	85
Law of Reflection, Projection, and Perspective	99
Law of Patience	113
Law of Attention	129
Law of Intention	145
Law of Abundance and Prosperity	161
Law of Karma	177
Law of Responsibility	193
Law of Forgiveness	209
Law of No Judgment	225
Law of Unconditional Love and Gratitude	241
Law of Oneness	257

Introduction

Practicing Love took readers beyond the "veil of consciousness" to a place of self-reflection and inner peace. It emphasized how finding love within ourselves is essential for transforming how we view our external world. It was about self-discovery and the importance of manifesting the vibration of love in our lives. Everything within and around us is energy. Understanding how we direct this energy, both positively and negatively, is the key to making dramatic changes in our lives. It is time for humanity to raise its collective consciousness through unconditional love and service to others.

Practicing Love helped you meditate with ease, turned your mind off to distractions, and opened your world of possibilities with easy tips for you to incorporate into your everyday busy life. It went into depth about how the ego makes you operate out of fear and showed you how to turn a negative mindset into one that empowers you to conquer obstacles by getting out of your comfort zone. It went through simple descriptions of all the universal laws that helped you live a more positive, happy, and fulfilled life. It gave you hundreds of affirmations to recite when you are feeling down in any scenario. It also showed you which words to eliminate from your vocabulary immediately and how to start talking in manifestation mode 24/7. It had tons of exercises to help you live in the present moment, become more patient, support yourself in forgiving yourself and others, become less selfish, not react out of judgement, and finally, to always feel unconditionally loved.

This gratitude journal will take you through all the spiritual laws of attraction and teach you how to show grace in your everyday lives.

To use it effectively, wake up every morning and say one thing you are grateful for. It could be something you want to manifest into existence, it could be someone you love, it could be for your health, it is about saying everything you could possibly want to say you are grateful for that day.

Next you will write down an affirmation you will want to repeat throughout the day. It could be something you want to work on, it could be something you need help reassuring yourself to believe in when you have doubts, or it could be a simple "I love myself."

After that, you can either write an excerpt in the journal, or you can wait until evening in case there is something you want to fulfill and talk about it. You can page through the prompts to whatever you want to write about, you don't have to go in order. If you aren't feeling a prompt, you can absolutely make up your own. They are only there to guide you and reflect.

May your life be filled with the vibration of love, and always remember to write from a place of gratitude.

Law of the Ego

Gratitude Entry #1

At the age of 18, I made up my mind to never have another bad day in my life. I dove into an endless sea of gratitude from which I've never emerged.
—Patch Adams

I'M GRATEFUL FOR _____

AFFIRMATION OF THE DAY:
_____

How have you broken through limitations your ego put on you?

_____
_____
_____
_____
_____
_____
_____
_____
_____
_____
_____
_____
_____
_____
_____
_____
_____
_____
_____
_____

Gratitude Entry #2

Gratitude helps you to grow and expand; gratitude brings joy and laughter into your life and into the lives of all those around you.
—Eileen Caddy

I'm grateful for_____

Affirmation of the day:
_____

Change five "I can'ts" into "I cans."

_____
_____
_____
_____
_____
_____

Gratitude Entry #3

The best way to pay for a lovely moment is to enjoy it.
—Richard Bach

I'm grateful for_____

Affirmation of the day:
_____

Write about what self-worth means to you.

_____
_____
_____
_____
_____
_____

Gratitude Entry #4

When gratitude becomes an essential foundation in our lives, miracles start to appear everywhere.
—Emmanuel Dagher

I'm grateful for _____

Affirmation of the day:
_____

Write about how you nourish and take care of your body.

_____
_____
_____
_____
_____
_____

Gratitude Entry #5

If the only prayer you said in your whole life was "thank you" that would suffice.
—Meister Eckhart

I'm grateful for _____

Affirmation of the day:
_____

Write how you are going to shed your ego and maximize your true potential.

_____
_____
_____
_____
_____
_____

GRATITUDE ENTRY #6

I have to have an attitude of gratitude and not miss opportunities.
—Urijah Faber

I'M GRATEFUL FOR_____

AFFIRMATION OF THE DAY:
_____

Write about a scary challenge or obstacle you didn't want to face, then bit the bullet, and realized anything was possible.

Gratitude Entry #7

Some people grumble that roses have thorns; I am grateful that thorns have roses.
—Alphonse Karr

I'm grateful for _____

Affirmation of the day:
_____

Write about a time you broke out of your comfort zone.

_____
_____
_____
_____
_____
_____
_____
_____
_____
_____
_____
_____
_____
_____
_____
_____
_____
_____
_____
_____
_____
_____

Gratitude Entry #8

May the gratitude in my heart kiss all the universe.
—Hafiz

I'M GRATEFUL FOR _____

AFFIRMATION OF THE DAY:
_____

List five negative words you use in your vocabulary and five positive words you are going to replace them with.

_____
_____
_____
_____
_____
_____

Gratitude Entry #9

When I started counting my blessings my whole life turned around.
—Willie Nelson

I'M GRATEFUL FOR _____

AFFIRMATION OF THE DAY:
_____

Write about five little victories you never celebrated but should have.

_____
_____
_____
_____
_____
_____

Gratitude Entry #10

To speak gratitude is courteous and pleasant, to enact gratitude is generous and noble, but to live gratitude is to touch Heaven.
—Johannes A. Gaertner

I'm grateful for_____

Affirmation of the day:
_____

What are five of your personality traits you are most thankful for and why?

_____
_____
_____
_____
_____
_____

Gratitude Entry #11

Stop now. Enjoy the moment. It's now or never.
—Maxime Lagacé

I'm grateful for_____

Affirmation of the day:
_____

What physical characteristics of yours are you most grateful for?

_____
_____
_____
_____
_____
_____

GRATITUDE ENTRY #12

Expectation has brought me disappointment. Disappointment has brought me wisdom. Acceptance, gratitude and appreciation have brought me joy and fulfillment.
—Rasheed Ogunlaru

I'M GRATEFUL FOR_____

AFFIRMATION OF THE DAY:
_____

Describe your happiest childhood memory.

_____
_____
_____
_____
_____
_____
_____
_____
_____
_____
_____
_____
_____
_____
_____
_____
_____
_____
_____
_____
_____
_____
_____
_____

Gratitude Entry #13

I've started to look at life differently. When you're thanking God for every little you- every meal, every time you wake up, every time you take a sip of water – you can't help but be more thankful for life itself, for the unlikely and miraculous fact that you exist at all.
—A.J. Jacobs

I'm grateful for_____

Affirmation of the day:

_____

What is the biggest lesson you learned in childhood? And why are you grateful for it now?

Gratitude Entry #14

Don't pray when it rains if you don't pray when the sun shines.
—Leroy "Satchel" Paige

I'M GRATEFUL FOR _____

AFFIRMATION OF THE DAY:
_____

List five talents you have that you are grateful for.

_____
_____
_____
_____
_____

Gratitude Entry #15

The dominant characteristic of an authentic spiritual life is the gratitude that flows from trust – not only for all the gifts that I receive from God, but gratitude for all the suffering. Because in that purifying experience, suffering has often been the shortest path to intimacy with God.
—Brennan Manning

I'M GRATEFUL FOR _____

AFFIRMATION OF THE DAY:
_____

List five leadership qualities you have and are grateful for.

_____
_____
_____
_____
_____

Gratitude Entry #16

If you count all your assets, you always show a profit.
—Robert Quillen

I'm grateful for _____

Affirmation of the day:

_____

List five skills you have that most people don't possess.

_____
_____
_____
_____
_____
_____

Gratitude Entry #17

'Grateful' is a small word to express my gratitude, as God has blessed me with so many opportunities to restart my life.
—Adnan Sami

I'm grateful for _____

Affirmation of the day:

_____

Describe a favorite outfit and why you feel great when wearing it.

_____
_____
_____
_____
_____
_____

Gratitude Entry #18

We have to fill our hearts with gratitude. Gratitude makes everything that we have more than enough.
—Susan L. Taylor

I'M GRATEFUL FOR_____

AFFIRMATION OF THE DAY:
_____

Write about a time when you felt courageous.

Gratitude Entry #19

We hope that, when the insects take over the world, they will remember with gratitude how we took them along on all our picnics.
—William Vaughn

I'm grateful for _____

Affirmation of the day:
_____

What makes you beautiful?

_____
_____
_____
_____
_____
_____
_____
_____
_____
_____
_____
_____
_____
_____
_____
_____
_____
_____
_____
_____

Gratitude Entry #20

God is always coming to you in the Sacrament of the Present Moment. Meet and receive Him there with gratitude in that sacrament.
—Evelyn Underhill

I'm grateful for _____

Affirmation of the day:
_____

One thing I appreciate about myself is…

_____
_____
_____
_____
_____
_____

Gratitude Entry #21

Happiness cannot be traveled to, owned, earned, worn or consumed. Happiness is a spiritual experience of living every minute with love, grace and gratitude.
—Denis Waitley

I'm grateful for _____

Affirmation of the day:
_____

Write about what makes you unique.

_____
_____
_____
_____
_____

Gratitude Entry #22

Going to religious places gives me clarity. When I am sitting here, I am in a state of gratitude with my defense mechanism down and am open to receiving that energy, that gives me clarity as at that time, you are listening to your heart. The heart shows you the direction in life. The mind exists only to execute your emotion.
—Arjun Rampal

I'M GRATEFUL FOR_____

AFFIRMATION OF THE DAY:

_____

What fear are you currently facing? How can you use this fear to your advantage?

Law of Manifestation

Gratitude Entry #23

I'm grateful to God for His bountiful gifts... He gave me courage and faith in myself.
—Loretta Young

I'M GRATEFUL FOR_____

AFFIRMATION OF THE DAY:
_____

Think of three times pure luck or grace has saved you. Write a paragraph about each and focus on who and how the events took place.

Gratitude Entry #24

A contented mind is the greatest blessing a man can enjoy in this world.
—Joseph Addison

I'M GRATEFUL FOR_____

AFFIRMATION OF THE DAY:
_____

List five things you are looking forward to in the next year.

_____
_____
_____
_____
_____

Gratitude Entry #25

The more you recognize and express gratitude for the things you have, the more things you will have to express gratitude for.
—Zig Ziglar

I'M GRATEFUL FOR_____

AFFIRMATION OF THE DAY:
_____

When you were a child, what did you want to be when you grew up?

_____
_____
_____
_____
_____
_____

Gratitude Entry #26

The mind is like a flower. It does not bloom without the lights of appreciation, encouragement and love.
—Debasish Mridha

I'm grateful for _____

Affirmation of the day:

_____

What is your top goal? Why is this goal important to you?

_____
_____
_____
_____
_____
_____

Gratitude Entry #27

Opening your eyes to more of the world around you can deeply enhance your gratitude practice.
—Derrick Carpenter

I'm grateful for _____

Affirmation of the day:

_____

List five things that you will conquer in the next year.

_____
_____
_____
_____
_____
_____

GRATITUDE ENTRY #28

To live a life fulfilled reflect on the things you have with gratitude.
—Jaren Davis

I'M GRATEFUL FOR _____

AFFIRMATION OF THE DAY:
_____

Write a thank you letter to the Universe of things you want to possess as if you already have them.

_____
_____
_____
_____
_____
_____
_____
_____
_____
_____
_____
_____
_____
_____
_____
_____
_____
_____
_____
_____
_____
_____

GRATITUDE ENTRY #29

Experience teaches us that we do not always receive the blessings we ask for in prayer.
—Mary Baker Eddy

I'M GRATEFUL FOR_____

AFFIRMATION OF THE DAY:
_____

List all the disharmonious behaviors you have and how you will be eliminating them from your life.

_____
_____
_____
_____
_____
_____
_____
_____
_____
_____
_____
_____
_____
_____
_____
_____
_____
_____
_____
_____
_____
_____

Gratitude Entry #30

Gratitude is more of a compliment to yourself than someone else.
—Raheel Farooq

I'm grateful for_____

Affirmation of the day:
_____

Write about a wish you had that came true.

_____
_____
_____
_____
_____
_____
_____

Gratitude Entry #31

May the work of your hands be a sign of gratitude and reverence to the human condition.
—Mahatma Gandhi

I'm grateful for_____

Affirmation of the day:
_____

What opportunities have changed your life?

_____
_____
_____
_____
_____
_____

Gratitude Entry #32

Gratitude is when memory is stored in the heart and not in the mind.
—Lionel Hampton

I'm grateful for _____

Affirmation of the day:
_____

Write about ideas you will create into your reality.

_____
_____
_____
_____
_____
_____
_____
_____

Gratitude Entry #33

The deepest craving of human nature is the need to be appreciated.
—William James

I'm grateful for _____

Affirmation of the day:
_____

Write how you overcame self-doubt.

_____
_____
_____
_____
_____
_____
_____

Gratitude Entry #34

If you want to find happiness, find gratitude.
—Steve Maraboli

I'm grateful for _____

Affirmation of the day:
_____

Write a clear vision of your plan so it can come into fruition.

_____
_____
_____
_____
_____
_____
_____
_____
_____
_____
_____
_____
_____
_____
_____
_____
_____
_____
_____
_____
_____
_____
_____

GRATITUDE ENTRY #35

Meditate, relax and just "be" for a moment. Remember that this moment is perfect the way it is and you don't need to change it.
—Maxime Lagacé

I'M GRATEFUL FOR_____

AFFIRMATION OF THE DAY:
_____

Write about a time the Universe came together and brought you the most magical gift in the most unforgettable way.

_____
_____
_____
_____
_____
_____
_____
_____
_____
_____
_____
_____
_____
_____
_____
_____
_____
_____
_____
_____
_____
_____

Gratitude Entry #36

I acknowledge my feeling and gratitude for life by praising the world and whoever made all these things.
—Mary Oliver

I'M GRATEFUL FOR_____

AFFIRMATION OF THE DAY:

Write about a time where you relinquished all control and your intuitive guidance took its course.

Gratitude Entry #37

When life is sweet, say thank you and celebrate. And when life is bitter, say thank you and grow.
—Shauna Niequist

I'M GRATEFUL FOR_____

AFFIRMATION OF THE DAY:

Write about a time you felt most fulfilled.

Gratitude Entry #38

It's wonderful to be grateful. To have that gratitude well out from deep within you and pour out in waves. Once you truly experience this, you will never want to give it up.
—Srikumar Rao

I'm grateful for _____

Affirmation of the day:
_____

Write about a time you were able to receive and left your negative back talk at the door.

_____
_____
_____
_____
_____
_____
_____

Gratitude Entry #39

Saying thank you is more than good manners. It is good spirituality.
—Alfred Painter

I'm grateful for _____

Affirmation of the day:
_____

Write about being a magnet to everything you are attracting.

_____
_____
_____
_____
_____
_____

GRATITUDE ENTRY #40

Gratitude is one of the sweet shortcuts to finding peace of mind and happiness inside. No matter what is going on outside of us, there's always something we could be grateful for.
—Barry Neil Kaufman

I'M GRATEFUL FOR_____

AFFIRMATION OF THE DAY:
_____

Write about your journey to fulfillment. If it hasn't happened, write as though it has. Smile and release.

_____
_____
_____
_____
_____
_____
_____
_____
_____
_____
_____
_____
_____
_____
_____
_____
_____
_____
_____
_____
_____
_____

Gratitude Entry #41

The way to develop the best that is in a person is by appreciation and encouragement.
—Charles Schwab

I'M GRATEFUL FOR _____

AFFIRMATION OF THE DAY:
_____

Write about your passion.

_____
_____
_____
_____
_____
_____
_____
_____
_____
_____
_____
_____
_____
_____
_____
_____
_____
_____
_____
_____
_____
_____

Gratitude Entry #42

The best way to show my gratitude to God is to accept everything, even my problems, with joy.
—Mother Teresa

I'm grateful for _____

Affirmation of the day:
_____

List all the ways you silence your mind when doubt creeps in.

_____
_____
_____
_____
_____

Gratitude Entry #43

Appreciation is a wonderful thing. It makes what is excellent in others belong to us as well.
—Voltaire

I'm grateful for _____

Affirmation of the day:
_____

List your "don't wants" and change them into saying what you "do want."

_____
_____
_____
_____
_____

Law of the Present Moment

Gratitude Entry #44

The more grateful I am, the more beauty I see.
—Mary Davis

I'M GRATEFUL FOR_____

AFFIRMATION OF THE DAY:
_____

Describe one thing you like about your daily commute to work?

_____
_____
_____
_____
_____
_____

Gratitude Entry #45

We can always find something to be thankful for, and there may be reasons why we ought to be thankful for even those dispensations which appear dark and frowning.
—Albert Barnes

I'M GRATEFUL FOR_____

AFFIRMATION OF THE DAY:
_____

Open your photo album and find one photo you like. Why are you grateful for this one?

_____
_____
_____
_____
_____
_____

Gratitude Entry #46

Gratitude turns what we have into enough.
—Aesop

I'm grateful for _____

Affirmation of the day:
_____

Describe your favorite thing about waking up in the morning.
_____
_____
_____
_____
_____
_____

Gratitude Entry #47

I have had friends who have acted kindly toward me, and it has been my good fortune to have it in my power to give them substantial proofs of gratitude.
—Giacomo Casanova

I'm grateful for _____

Affirmation of the day:
_____

What sounds can you hear right now that make you feel at peace?
_____
_____
_____
_____
_____
_____

GRATITUDE ENTRY #48

Be grateful for what you have and stop complaining – it bores everybody else, does you no good, and doesn't solve any problems.
—Zig Ziglar

I'M GRATEFUL FOR_____

AFFIRMATION OF THE DAY:
_____

What about nature are you grateful for?

_____
_____
_____
_____
_____
_____
_____
_____
_____
_____
_____
_____
_____
_____
_____
_____
_____
_____
_____
_____
_____
_____

Gratitude Entry #49

Happiness cannot be traveled to, owned, earned, worn or consumed. Happiness is the spiritual experience of living every minute with love, grace, and gratitude.
—Denis Waitley

I'M GRATEFUL FOR _____

AFFIRMATION OF THE DAY:
_____

What is one thing you've learned this week that you're thankful for?

_____
_____
_____
_____
_____
_____
_____
_____
_____
_____
_____
_____
_____
_____
_____
_____
_____
_____
_____
_____

Gratitude Entry #50

If you can write any way and it's working out, just bow down in gratitude.
—Jennifer Egan

I'M GRATEFUL FOR_____

AFFIRMATION OF THE DAY:
_____

List five things you are doing well currently and how.

_____
_____
_____
_____
_____
_____

Gratitude Entry #51

Let us swell with gratitude and allow it to overwhelm us. It isn't as cliché as we make it; life truly is short. Let's spend it all lavishly wallowing in gratitude.
—Grace Gealey

I'M GRATEFUL FOR_____

AFFIRMATION OF THE DAY:
_____

What has been the highlight of your day today?

_____
_____
_____
_____
_____
_____

Gratitude Entry #52

I acknowledge with great gratitude the peace and contentment we can find for ourselves in the spiritual cocoons of our homes, our sacrament meetings, and our holy temples.
—James E. Faust

I'm grateful for_____

Affirmation of the day:
_____

List five things you love about your home.

_____
_____
_____
_____
_____
_____

Gratitude Entry #53

Find the good and praise it. Give thanks for a little and you will find a lot.
—Hansa Proverb

I'm grateful for_____

Affirmation of the day:
_____

How can you pamper yourself in the next 24 hours?

_____
_____
_____
_____
_____

Gratitude Entry #54

Of the blessings set before you, make your choice, and be content.
—Samuel Johnson

I'm grateful for _____

Affirmation of the day:
_____

Describe a recent time when you truly felt at peace.

_____
_____
_____
_____
_____
_____
_____
_____
_____
_____
_____
_____
_____
_____
_____
_____
_____
_____
_____
_____
_____
_____
_____

GRATITUDE ENTRY #55

So much has been given to me; I have no time to ponder over that which has been denied.
—Helen Keller

I'M GRATEFUL FOR_____

AFFIRMATION OF THE DAY:
_____

When was the last walk you went on? What parts of nature did you not notice before that brought you joy?

_____
_____
_____
_____
_____
_____
_____
_____
_____
_____
_____
_____
_____
_____
_____
_____
_____
_____
_____
_____

Gratitude Entry #56

I thank everything, because everything teaches me something.
—Maxime Lagacé

I'M GRATEFUL FOR_____

AFFIRMATION OF THE DAY:
_____

Write about a time you belly laughed so hard you may have peed your pants.

_____
_____
_____
_____
_____
_____

Gratitude Entry #57

Those with a grateful mindset tend to see the message in the mess. And even though life may knock them down, the grateful find reasons, if even small ones, to get up.
—Steve Maraboli

I'M GRATEFUL FOR_____

AFFIRMATION OF THE DAY:
_____

Write about your favorite food and the joy it brings to you.

_____
_____
_____
_____
_____
_____

Gratitude Entry #58

The essence of all beautiful art is gratitude.
—Friedrich Nietzsche

I'M GRATEFUL FOR _____

AFFIRMATION OF THE DAY:

_____

Write a story about the stars in the sky.

_____
_____
_____
_____
_____
_____
_____

Gratitude Entry #59

When you are grateful – when you can see what you have – you unlock blessings to flow in your life.
—Suze Orman

I'M GRATEFUL FOR _____

AFFIRMATION OF THE DAY:

_____

Write about the best workout you ever had.

_____
_____
_____
_____
_____
_____

GRATITUDE ENTRY #60

I'm in a constant state of gratitude.
—Mandy Patinkin

I'M GRATEFUL FOR _____

AFFIRMATION OF THE DAY:
_____

Take a moment to focus on all your sensations and write about all of them.

_____
_____
_____
_____
_____
_____
_____
_____
_____
_____
_____
_____
_____
_____
_____
_____
_____
_____
_____
_____
_____
_____
_____
_____
_____
_____

Gratitude Entry #61

Showing gratitude is one of the simplest yet most powerful things humans can do for each other.
—Randy Pausch

I'm grateful for_____

Affirmation of the day:

_____

List all the things you appreciate.

Gratitude Entry #62

Nature's beauty is a gift that cultivates appreciation and gratitude.
—Louie Schwartzberg

I'M GRATEFUL FOR_____

AFFIRMATION OF THE DAY:
_____

List all the positive things that help calm your anxiety.

_____
_____
_____
_____
_____
_____
_____

Gratitude Entry #63

In everything, give thanks.
—Thessalonians 5:18

I'M GRATEFUL FOR_____

AFFIRMATION OF THE DAY:
_____

What inspirational content have you read that made you feel motivated?

_____
_____
_____
_____
_____
_____
_____

Gratitude Entry #64

Gratitude for the seemingly insignificant—a seed—this plants the giant miracle.
—Ann Voskamp

I'm grateful for _____

Affirmation of the day:
_____

Write about a time you unplugged from all digital distractions and how it made you feel alive.

_____
_____
_____
_____
_____
_____

Gratitude Entry #65

Thank you is the best prayer that anyone could say. I say that one a lot. Thank you expresses extreme gratitude, humility, understanding.
—Alice Walker

I'm grateful for _____

Affirmation of the day:
_____

Write about a time you jammed out and danced for no reason at all.

_____
_____
_____
_____
_____
_____

Law of Free Will

Gratitude Entry #66

Our favorite attitude should be gratitude.
—Zig Ziglar

I'm grateful for _____

Affirmation of the day:
_____

How are you directing your own path?

_____
_____
_____
_____
_____
_____
_____

Gratitude Entry #67

Gratitude is the sign of noble souls.
—Aesop

I'm grateful for _____

Affirmation of the day:
_____

Write about a time when you didn't care what anybody else thought.

_____
_____
_____
_____
_____
_____
_____

Gratitude Entry #68

So every single day, I found something to be grateful for and that's a powerful lesson.
—Alice Barrett

I'm grateful for _____

Affirmation of the day:

_____

Write about how you raise people up instead of cutting them down.

_____
_____
_____
_____
_____
_____
_____

Gratitude Entry #69

I would maintain that thanks are the highest form of thought, and that gratitude is happiness doubled by wonder.
—G.K. Chesterton

I'm grateful for _____

Affirmation of the day:

_____

What is your heart telling you?

_____
_____
_____
_____
_____
_____

GRATITUDE ENTRY #70

Through the eyes of gratitude, everything is a miracle.
—Mary Davis

I'M GRATEFUL FOR _____

AFFIRMATION OF THE DAY:
_____

What experience expanded your consciousness and brought you closer to the truth?

_____
_____
_____
_____
_____
_____
_____
_____
_____
_____
_____
_____
_____
_____
_____
_____
_____
_____
_____
_____
_____
_____
_____
_____

GRATITUDE ENTRY #71

The world has enough beautiful mountains and meadows, spectacular skies and serene lakes. It has enough lush forests, flowered fields, and sandy beaches. It has plenty of stars and the promise of a new sunrise and sunset every day. What the world needs more of is people to appreciate and enjoy it.
—Michael Josephson

I'M GRATEFUL FOR _____

AFFIRMATION OF THE DAY:
_____

How are you going to change your reality by shifting your belief system to serve your higher purpose?

Gratitude Entry #72

As with all commandments, gratitude is a description of a successful mode of living. The thankful heart opens our eyes to a multitude of blessings that continually surround us.
—James E. Faust

I'm grateful for _____

Affirmation of the day:
_____

What path forces you into a positive mindset?

_____
_____
_____
_____
_____
_____

Gratitude Entry #73

Wake at dawn with a winged heart and give thanks for another day of loving.
—Kahlil Gibran

I'm grateful for _____

Affirmation of the day:
_____

Where will you go with your free will to see your ultimate potential?

_____
_____
_____
_____
_____
_____

Gratitude Entry #74

To come to terms with our beginning requires a truthful story to acquire the skills to live in gratitude rather than resentment for the gift of life.
—Stanley Hauerwas

I'm grateful for _____

Affirmation of the day:

_____

What was something you did for the first time recently?

_____
_____
_____
_____
_____
_____

Gratitude Entry #75

There are only two ways to live your life. One is as though nothing is a miracle. The other is as though everything is a miracle.
—Albert Einstein

I'm grateful for _____

Affirmation of the day:

_____

What makes you happy when you're feeling down?

_____
_____
_____
_____
_____
_____

Gratitude Entry #76

When you are thankful or you feel appreciation, you are in the ultimate state to receive. When you embrace gratitude, your body as the unconscious mind will begin to believe it is in that future reality in the present moment.
—Dr. Joe Dispenza

I'M GRATEFUL FOR_____

AFFIRMATION OF THE DAY:
_____

What do you love and cherish?

_____
_____
_____
_____
_____
_____
_____
_____
_____
_____
_____
_____
_____
_____
_____
_____
_____
_____
_____
_____
_____
_____

Gratitude Entry #77

The roots of all goodness lie in the soil of appreciation for goodness.
—Dalai Lama

I'm grateful for _____

Affirmation of the day:
_____

Describe a "perfect day" you recently had.

Gratitude Entry #78

Free yourself from the complexities and drama of your life. Simplify. Look within. Within ourselves we all have the gifts and talents we need to fulfill the purpose we've been blessed with.
—Steve Maraboli

I'm grateful for_____

Affirmation of the day:
_____

What modern inventions are you thankful for?

_____
_____
_____
_____
_____
_____

Gratitude Entry #79

Feeling grateful or appreciative of someone or something in your life actually attracts more of the things that you appreciate and value into your life.
—Christiane Northrup

I'm grateful for_____

Affirmation of the day:
_____

What is something that cheers you up on a rough day?

_____
_____
_____
_____
_____
_____

Gratitude Entry #80

The single dynamic that helps people be most aware of God and most experiencing the fruit of the Spirit is gratitude.
—John Ortberg

I'm grateful for_____

Affirmation of the day:
_____

What is the best thing that happened to you this week?

_____
_____
_____
_____
_____

Gratitude Entry #81

Gratitude is the appreciation of things that are not deserved, earned or demanded – those wonderful things that we take for granted.
—Renee Paule

I'm grateful for_____

Affirmation of the day:
_____

How do you strive to make every single day better?

_____
_____
_____
_____
_____
_____

Gratitude Entry #82

The world gives you way more than you ever give it.
—Kamal Ravikant

I'm grateful for _____

Affirmation of the day:

_____

Write about a glorious time you exercised the power of choice.

Gratitude Entry #83

Think with great gratitude of those who have lighted the flame within us.
—Albert Schweitzer

I'm grateful for _____

Affirmation of the day:

_____

Write about a time you took yourself out of a negative situation and how you took control.

Gratitude Entry #84

I have to read something positive every single day. I have to have faith that the day is unfolding in a way that is going to be useful to somebody else... For me, living every day in gratitude has been profound for me.
—Lea Thompson

I'M GRATEFUL FOR _____

AFFIRMATION OF THE DAY:
_____

Pretend you are a blank canvas. How are you starting over?

_____
_____
_____
_____
_____
_____

Gratitude Entry #85

I write about art out of gratitude to painters for the joy and spiritual uplift they have given me. Painters interpret for us the visual glories of God and, in this way, bring us closer to Him.
—Susan Vreeland

I'M GRATEFUL FOR _____

AFFIRMATION OF THE DAY:
_____

List five things that always put a smile on your face.

_____
_____
_____
_____
_____
_____

Gratitude Entry #86

The struggle ends when gratitude begins.
—Neale Donald Walsch

I'm grateful for _____

Affirmation of the day:
_____

What is your favorite emotion to feel?

_____
_____
_____
_____
_____
_____
_____

Gratitude Entry #87

Among the things you can give and still keep are your word, a smile, and a grateful heart.
—Zig Ziglar

I'm grateful for _____

Affirmation of the day:
_____

What makes you happy to be alive?

_____
_____
_____
_____
_____
_____

Law of Relativity

Gratitude Entry #88

This is a wonderful day. I've never seen this one before.
—Maya Angelou

I'M GRATEFUL FOR_____

AFFIRMATION OF THE DAY:
_____

What lessons have you received that strengthened your light within?

GRATITUDE ENTRY #89

Gratitude unlocks the fullness of life.
—Melody Beattie

I'M GRATEFUL FOR _____

AFFIRMATION OF THE DAY:
_____

What negative thoughts have you given too much meaning to that you get to turn into positive thoughts?

_____
_____
_____
_____
_____
_____
_____
_____
_____
_____
_____
_____
_____
_____
_____
_____
_____
_____
_____
_____
_____

Gratitude Entry #90

When it comes to life the critical thing is whether you take things for granted or take them with gratitude.
—G.K. Chesterton

I'M GRATEFUL FOR_____

AFFIRMATION OF THE DAY:
_____

List five ways you are fortunate.

_____
_____
_____
_____
_____
_____

Gratitude Entry #91

Things must be felt with the heart.
—Helen Keller

I'M GRATEFUL FOR_____

AFFIRMATION OF THE DAY:
_____

List five items you take for granted, which might not be available to people in other parts of the world.

_____
_____
_____
_____
_____
_____

Gratitude Entry #92

I awoke this morning with devout thanksgiving for my friends, the old and the new.
—Ralph Waldo Emerson

I'm grateful for _____

Affirmation of the day:
_____

What freedoms are you most grateful for?

_____
_____
_____
_____
_____
_____

Gratitude Entry #93

A grateful heart is a beginning of greatness. It is an expression of humility. It is a foundation for the development of such virtues as prayer, faith, courage, contentment, happiness, love, and well-being.
—James E. Faust

I'm grateful for _____

Affirmation of the day:
_____

What luxury are you lucky to have access to?

_____
_____
_____
_____
_____
_____

GRATITUDE ENTRY #94

Gratitude is not a limited resource, nor is it costly. It is abundant as air. We breathe it in but forget to exhale.
—Marshall Goldsmith

I'M GRATEFUL FOR_____

AFFIRMATION OF THE DAY:
_____

Write a Best List. The best you, the best everything and whatever that word means to you.

_____
_____
_____
_____
_____
_____
_____
_____
_____
_____
_____
_____
_____
_____
_____
_____
_____
_____
_____
_____
_____
_____
_____
_____

GRATITUDE ENTRY #95

Give thanks for a little and you will find a lot.
—Hansa Proverb

I'M GRATEFUL FOR_____

AFFIRMATION OF THE DAY:
_____

What amazing lessons did you learn from comparing things in a positive light?

_____
_____
_____
_____
_____
_____
_____
_____
_____
_____
_____
_____
_____
_____
_____
_____
_____
_____
_____
_____

Gratitude Entry #96

At times our own light goes out and is rekindled by a spark from another person. Each of us has cause to think with deep gratitude of those who have lighted the flame with in us.
—Albert Schweitzer

I'm grateful for _____

Affirmation of the day:
_____

How have you turned a "that's not fair" scenario into a triumph?

_____
_____
_____
_____
_____
_____

Gratitude Entry #97

A single grateful thought toward heaven is the most complete prayer.
—Gotthold Ephraim Lessing

I'm grateful for _____

Affirmation of the day:
_____

What are the five most important things in your life?

_____
_____
_____
_____
_____
_____

Gratitude Entry #98

Gratitude is what we radiate when we experience grace, and the soul was made to run on grace the way a 747 runs on rocket fuel.
—John Ortberg

I'm grateful for _____

Affirmation of the day:
_____

What's one way you used to compare yourself to others, but laugh about that now?

_____
_____
_____
_____
_____
_____

Gratitude Entry #99

Prayers of gratitude are powerful tools for wellness.
—Christiane Northrop

I'm grateful for _____

Affirmation of the day:
_____

Write about what clean water means to you.

_____
_____
_____
_____
_____
_____

Gratitude Entry #100

Make it a habit to tell people thank you. To express your appreciation, sincerely and without the expectation of anything in return. Truly appreciate those around you, and you'll soon find many others around you. Truly appreciate life, and you'll find that you have more of it.
—Ralph Marston

I'm grateful for _____

Affirmation of the day:
_____

Why is it more fulfilling to have love in your life than power?

Gratitude Entry #101

Never lose the childlike wonder show gratitude…Don't complain; just work harder…Never give up.
—Randy Pausch

I'M GRATEFUL FOR_____

AFFIRMATION OF THE DAY:
_____

Pretend there is no money, how would you live your life?

_____
_____
_____
_____
_____
_____
_____
_____
_____
_____
_____
_____
_____
_____
_____
_____
_____
_____
_____

Gratitude Entry #102

Change your expectation for appreciation and the world changes instantly.
—Tony Robbins

I'm grateful for _____

Affirmation of the day:

_____

Write about living like a carefree dog who feels unconditional love for everyone.

_____
_____
_____
_____
_____
_____

Gratitude Entry #103

Often people ask how I manage to be happy despite having no arms no legs. The quick answer is that I have a choice. I can be angry about not having limbs, or I can be thankful that I have a purpose. I chose gratitude.
—Nick Vujicic

I'm grateful for _____

Affirmation of the day:

_____

Compare compassion with empathy.

_____
_____
_____
_____
_____
_____

Gratitude Entry #104

If the only prayer you said in your whole life was, 'thank you,' that would suffice.
—Eckhart Tolle

I'm grateful for _____

Affirmation of the day:
_____

List something good that has recently caught your attention to make you realize how fortunate you are.

_____
_____
_____
_____
_____
_____

Gratitude Entry #105

As we express our gratitude, we must never forget that the highest appreciation is not to utter words, but to live by them.
—John F. Kennedy

I'm grateful for _____

Affirmation of the day:
_____

Write about people who first come to mind that don't have it as good as you do.

_____
_____
_____
_____
_____
_____

Gratitude Entry #106

Though I am grateful for the blessings of wealth, it hasn't changed who I am. My feet are still on the ground. I'm just wearing better shoes.
—Oprah Winfrey

I'M GRATEFUL FOR _____

AFFIRMATION OF THE DAY:
_____

Write about a day when you focused on positive thoughts and the good things that came from it.

GRATITUDE ENTRY #107

Gratitude is the healthiest of all human emotions. The more you express gratitude for what you have, the more likely you will have even more to express gratitude for.
—Zig Ziglar

I'M GRATEFUL FOR_____

AFFIRMATION OF THE DAY:
_____

How have you overcome putting pressure on yourself?

_____
_____
_____
_____
_____
_____
_____
_____
_____
_____
_____
_____
_____
_____
_____
_____
_____
_____
_____
_____

GRATITUDE ENTRY #108

I work very hard, and I play very hard. I'm grateful for life. And I live it – I believe life loves the liver of it. I live it.
—Maya Angelou

I'M GRATEFUL FOR_____

AFFIRMATION OF THE DAY:
_____

What are things that make you happy to relate to?

_____
_____
_____
_____
_____
_____
_____
_____
_____
_____
_____
_____
_____
_____
_____
_____
_____
_____
_____
_____

Law of Resistance, Attachment, and Detachment

Gratitude Entry #109

I was a pain most of my childhood, always mad at the things I didn't have. Things shifted drastically in my 20s when I started putting an emphasis on gratitude. Focus on the good you do have, not the things you lack.
—Lewis Howes

I'M GRATEFUL FOR _____

AFFIRMATION OF THE DAY:
_____

Write about a time when you faced your fear head on.

_____
_____
_____
_____
_____
_____
_____
_____
_____
_____
_____
_____
_____
_____
_____
_____
_____
_____
_____
_____
_____
_____

Gratitude Entry #110

Now is no time to think of what you do not have. Think of what you can do with what there is.
—Ernest Hemingway

I'm grateful for _____

Affirmation of the day:
_____

How do you detach from an outcome so as to not have doubt?

_____
_____
_____
_____
_____
_____

Gratitude Entry #111

You pray in your distress and in your need; would that you might pray also in the fullness of your joy and in your days of abundance.
—Kahlil Gibran

I'm grateful for _____

Affirmation of the day:
_____

When was a situation you let the negative flow right through you without resistance or affecting you?

_____
_____
_____
_____
_____
_____

Gratitude Entry #112

I was complaining that I had no shoes till I met a man who had no feet.
—Confucius

I'm grateful for _____

Affirmation of the day:
_____

When was a time you had wisdom to not change a situation but walk away without wasting mental or physical energy?

_____
_____
_____
_____
_____
_____

Gratitude Entry #113

In order to attract more of the blessings that life has to offer, you must truly appreciate what you already have.
—Ralph Marston

I'm grateful for _____

Affirmation of the day:
_____

How will you approach situations you cannot change in a positive manner?

_____
_____
_____
_____
_____
_____

Gratitude Entry #114

Give yourself a gift of five minutes of contemplation in awe of everything you see around you. Go outside and turn your attention to the many miracles around you. This five-minute-a-day regimen of appreciation and gratitude will help you to focus your life in awe.
—Wayne Dyer

I'M GRATEFUL FOR

AFFIRMATION OF THE DAY:

Write about a time you finally broke free from attachment.

Gratitude Entry #115

The debt of gratitude we owe our mother and father goes forward, not backward. What we owe our parents is the bill presented to us by our children.
—Nancy Friday

I'M GRATEFUL FOR_____

AFFIRMATION OF THE DAY:
_____

Name a time you finally detached from an outcome and the Universe provided.

_____
_____
_____
_____
_____
_____
_____
_____
_____
_____
_____
_____
_____
_____
_____
_____
_____
_____
_____
_____

Gratitude Entry #116

Gratitude opens the door to the power, the wisdom, the creativity of the universe. You open the door through gratitude.
—Deepak Chopra

I'm grateful for _____

Affirmation of the day:
_____

Write about a time when you searched for a solution instead of simply complaining about your situation.

_____
_____
_____
_____
_____
_____

Gratitude Entry #117

Gratitude is an antidote to negative emotions, a neutralizer of envy, hostility, worry, and irritation. It is savoring; it is not taking things for granted; it is present oriented.
—Sonja Lyubomirsky

I'm grateful for _____

Affirmation of the day:
_____

Write about how you find good in every situation.

_____
_____
_____
_____
_____
_____

Gratitude Entry #118

If you only say one prayer in a day, make it thank you.
—Rumi

I'M GRATEFUL FOR _____

AFFIRMATION OF THE DAY:

_____

Write about a time you removed the power of your emotions and stayed strong.

_____
_____
_____
_____
_____
_____
_____

Gratitude Entry #119

What I've learned is there's a scientifically proven phenomenon that's attached to gratitude, and that if you consciously take not of what is good in your life, quantifiable benefits happen.
—Deborah Norville

I'M GRATEFUL FOR _____

AFFIRMATION OF THE DAY:

_____

How have you overcome being too hard on yourself with grace?

_____
_____
_____
_____
_____
_____

Gratitude Entry #120

Of all the characteristics needed for both a happy and morally decent life, none surpasses gratitude. Grateful people are happier, and grateful people are more morally decent.
—Dennis Prager

I'M GRATEFUL FOR _____

AFFIRMATION OF THE DAY:
_____

Write about all the beauty you let into your life.

_____
_____
_____
_____
_____
_____
_____
_____
_____
_____
_____
_____
_____
_____
_____
_____
_____
_____
_____
_____

GRATITUDE ENTRY #121

If you have your health, if you have people in your life to love, you are blessed. Slow down and enjoy the simple things in life.
—Joel Osteen

I'M GRATEFUL FOR _____

AFFIRMATION OF THE DAY:
_____

Write the top five things in your life that cause you stress. For each stress factor, write what you can do to change it.

_____
_____
_____
_____
_____
_____
_____
_____
_____
_____
_____
_____
_____
_____
_____
_____
_____
_____
_____
_____
_____

Gratitude Entry #122

I'm grateful for always this moment, the now, no matter what form it takes.
—Eckhart Tolle

I'm grateful for _____

Affirmation of the day:

_____

One thing that was a disappointment at the time, but turned out to be a blessing in disguise was. . .

_____
_____
_____
_____
_____
_____

Gratitude Entry #123

The greatest blessings of mankind are within us and within our reach. A wise man is content with his lot, whatever it may be, without wishing for what he has not.
—Seneca

I'm grateful for _____

Affirmation of the day:

_____

In contrast to one of my hardest days, I am grateful for today because. . .

_____
_____
_____
_____
_____
_____

Gratitude Entry #124

Gratitude makes sense of our past, brings peace for today, and creates a vision for tomorrow.
—Melody Beattie

I'M GRATEFUL FOR_____

AFFIRMATION OF THE DAY:
_____

Write about a challenging person in your life and the qualities you like about this person.

_____
_____
_____
_____
_____
_____

Gratitude Entry #125

Let gratitude be the pillow upon which you kneel to say your nightly prayer. And let faith be the bridge you build to overcome evil and welcome good.
—Maya Angelou

I'M GRATEFUL FOR_____

AFFIRMATION OF THE DAY:
_____

How did it feel to leave a bad situation?

_____
_____
_____
_____
_____
_____

GRATITUDE ENTRY #126

The loving parts of your personality have no trouble loving. That is all they do. You experience the loving parts of as gratitude, appreciation, caring, patience, contentment and awe of life.
—Gary Zukav

I'M GRATEFUL FOR_____

AFFIRMATION OF THE DAY:
_____

Write about a difficult experience that you learned from.

_____
_____
_____
_____
_____
_____
_____
_____
_____
_____
_____
_____
_____
_____
_____
_____
_____
_____
_____
_____
_____

Gratitude Entry #127

What you focus on expands, and when you focus on the goodness in your life, you create more of it. Opportunities, relationships, even money flowed my way when I learned to be grateful no matter what happened in my life.
—Oprah Winfrey

I'M GRATEFUL FOR_____

AFFIRMATION OF THE DAY:
_____

What have you learned from unpleasant emotions? And how have you turned those feelings around?

_____
_____
_____
_____
_____
_____
_____
_____
_____
_____
_____
_____
_____
_____
_____
_____
_____
_____
_____
_____
_____

Gratitude Entry #128

Gratitude is a powerful process for shifting your energy and bringing more of what you want into your life. Be grateful for what you already have and you will attract more good things.
—Rhonda Byrne

I'm grateful for _____

Affirmation of the day:
_____

Who or what in your life are you happy to have let go?

_____
_____
_____
_____
_____
_____

Gratitude Entry #129

Gratitude bestows reverence, allowing us to encounter everyday epiphanies, those transcendent moments of awe that change forever how we experience life and the world.
—John Milton

I'm grateful for _____

Affirmation of the day:
_____

How are you generating happiness from within?

_____
_____
_____
_____
_____
_____

Law of Reflection, Projection, and Perspective

Gratitude Entry #130

When you have balance in your life, work becomes an entirely different experience. There is a passion that moves you to a whole new level of fulfillment and gratitude, and that's when you can do your best… for yourself and for others.
—Cara Delevingne

I'M GRATEFUL FOR _____

AFFIRMATION OF THE DAY:
_____

How are you going to view the world as a happy place?

_____
_____
_____
_____
_____
_____

Gratitude Entry #131

You cannot do a kindness too soon because you never know how soon it will be too late.
—Ralph Waldo Emerson

I'M GRATEFUL FOR _____

AFFIRMATION OF THE DAY:
_____

How are you going to make sure your visualizations match your affirmations today?

_____
_____
_____
_____
_____
_____

Gratitude Entry #132

When you know in your bones that your body is a sacred gift, you move in the world with an effortless grace. Gratitude and humility rise up spontaneously.
—Debbie Ford

I'm grateful for _____

Affirmation of the day:
_____

List five things that made you happy today.

_____
_____
_____
_____
_____

Gratitude Entry #133

There is something calming and emotionally restoring when you focus on gratitude for a known deed that helped you, instead of fear of the unknown.
—Mark Goulston

I'm grateful for _____

Affirmation of the day:
_____

Who are you? Use inspirational words to describe yourself.

_____
_____
_____
_____
_____

Gratitude Entry #134

Cultivate the habit of being grateful for every good thing that comes to you, and to give thanks continuously. And because all things have contributed to your advancement, you should include all things in your gratitude.
—Ralph Waldo Emerson

I'M GRATEFUL FOR _____

AFFIRMATION OF THE DAY:
_____

When were you last encouraged/praised? Describe.

_____
_____
_____
_____
_____
_____
_____
_____
_____
_____
_____
_____
_____
_____
_____
_____
_____
_____
_____
_____

GRATITUDE ENTRY #135

When you give and carry out acts of kindness, it's as though something inside your body responds and says, 'Yes, this is how I ought to feel.
—Rabbi Harold Kushner

I'M GRATEFUL FOR _____

AFFIRMATION OF THE DAY:
_____

What was the biggest negative quality you saw in others that you found in yourself? How did you embrace and fix it? How are you grateful it is no longer a part of you?

_____
_____
_____
_____
_____
_____
_____
_____
_____
_____
_____
_____
_____
_____
_____
_____
_____
_____
_____
_____

Gratitude Entry #136

I lay my head down every night with a ton of gratitude.
—Ryan Leaf

I'm grateful for_____

Affirmation of the day:
_____

What do other people like about you?

_____
_____
_____
_____
_____
_____

Gratitude Entry #137

In our daily lives, we must see that it is not happiness that makes us grateful, but the gratefulness that makes us happy.
—Albert Clarke

I'm grateful for_____

Affirmation of the day:
_____

What is one lesson you learn from rude people? When they are rude, how can you stay calm and polite?

_____
_____
_____
_____
_____
_____

Gratitude Entry #138

Gratitude is the wine for the soul. Go on. Get drunk.
—Rumi

I'm grateful for _____

Affirmation of the day:
_____

What is something positive you can learn from one of your negative qualities?

_____
_____
_____
_____
_____
_____

Gratitude Entry #139

I really feel gratitude every day in my life that I'm able to do what I love, and I think, because I have that passion and spirit, I've had success.
—Christen Press

I'm grateful for _____

Affirmation of the day:
_____

What is a personal viewpoint that positively defines you as a person?

_____
_____
_____
_____
_____

Gratitude Entry #140

The only true and lasting inspiration for life is genuine love for God, and submitted gratitude that I get to be a part of the redemptive quest.
—John Ortberg

I'M GRATEFUL FOR_____

AFFIRMATION OF THE DAY:
_____

What was the biggest negative quality you saw in others that you found in yourself? How did you embrace and fix it?

_____
_____
_____
_____
_____
_____
_____
_____
_____
_____
_____
_____
_____
_____
_____
_____
_____
_____
_____
_____

GRATITUDE ENTRY #141

Gratitude can transform common days into thanksgivings, turn routine jobs into joy, and change ordinary opportunities into blessings.
—William Arthur Ward

I'M GRATEFUL FOR_____

AFFIRMATION OF THE DAY:
_____

How have you overcome your deep-seated feelings of resentment?

_____
_____
_____
_____
_____
_____
_____
_____
_____
_____
_____
_____
_____
_____
_____
_____
_____
_____
_____
_____
_____
_____

Gratitude Entry #142

It is through gratitude for the present moment that the spiritual dimensions of life opens up.
—Eckhart Tolle

I'M GRATEFUL FOR _____

AFFIRMATION OF THE DAY:
_____

How can you view your outer world in a positive light so it reflects and projects your higher self?

_____
_____
_____
_____
_____
_____
_____

Gratitude Entry #143

Gratitude is one of the strongest and most transformative states of being. It shifts your perspective from lack to abundance and allows you to focus on the good in your life, which in turn pulls more goodness into your reality.
—Jen Sincero

I'M GRATEFUL FOR _____

AFFIRMATION OF THE DAY:
_____

What do you admire in others that you see in yourself?

_____
_____
_____
_____
_____
_____
_____

Gratitude Entry #144

Gratitude is a currency that we can mint for ourselves, and spend without fear of bankruptcy.
—Fred De Witt Van Amburgh

I'M GRATEFUL FOR_____

AFFIRMATION OF THE DAY:
_____

If everyone is you, and you are everyone, how will you reflect gratitude throughout your day?

_____
_____
_____
_____
_____
_____

Gratitude Entry #145

I don't have to chase extraordinary moments to find happiness – it's right in front of me if I'm paying attention and practicing gratitude.
—Brené Brown

I'M GRATEFUL FOR_____

AFFIRMATION OF THE DAY:
_____

How are you positively creating your reality today?

_____
_____
_____
_____
_____
_____

Gratitude Entry #146

It has been said that life has treated me harshly; and sometimes I have complained in my heart because many pleasures of human experience have been withheld from me...if much has been denied me, much, very much, has been given me.
—Helen Keller

I'm grateful for _____

Affirmation of the day:
_____

Think of three people who irritate you or you have trouble getting along with. List three positive qualities about each person.

Gratitude Entry #147

Reflect upon your present blessings, of which every man has plenty; not on your past misfortunes, of which all men have some.
—Charles Dickens

I'm grateful for _____

Affirmation of the day:
_____

What are you going to create today?

_____
_____
_____
_____
_____

Gratitude Entry #148

Expressing gratitude is a natural state of being and reminds us that we are all connected.
—Valerie Elster

I'm grateful for _____

Affirmation of the day:
_____

What persona do you want to project?

_____
_____
_____
_____
_____
_____

Gratitude Entry #149

As long as this exists, this sunshine and this cloudless sky, and as long as I can enjoy it, how can I be sad?
—Anne Frank

I'm grateful for _____

Affirmation of the day:
_____

Does what I see in others belong in me?

_____
_____
_____
_____
_____
_____

Gratitude Entry #150

Embrace your life journey with gratitude, so that how you travel your path is more important than reaching your ultimate destination.
—Rosalene Glickman

I'm grateful for _____

Affirmation of the day:
_____

How do you reflect positively in negative situations?

_____
_____
_____
_____
_____
_____

Law of Patience

Gratitude Entry #151

Thou who has given so much to me, give me one more thing...a grateful heart!
—George Herbert

I'M GRATEFUL FOR_____

AFFIRMATION OF THE DAY:
_____

When were you most grateful because you practiced patience?

Gratitude Entry #152

I try to be grateful for the abundance of the blessings that I have, for the journey that I'm on and to relish each day as a gift.
—James McGreevey

I'm grateful for _____

Affirmation of the day:
_____

When did having patience pay off?

_____
_____
_____
_____
_____
_____
_____
_____
_____
_____
_____
_____
_____
_____
_____
_____
_____
_____
_____
_____

Gratitude Entry #153

A person however learned and qualified in his life's work in whom gratitude is absent, is devoid of that beauty of character which makes personality fragrant.
—Hazrat Inayat Khan

I'm grateful for_____

Affirmation of the day:
_____

What helps you relax?

_____
_____
_____
_____
_____
_____

Gratitude Entry #154

Let us be grateful to the people who make us happy; they are the charming gardeners who make our souls blossom.
—Marcel Proust

I'm grateful for_____

Affirmation of the day:
_____

One way I have been trying to slow down is _____, and it has allowed me to appreciate. . .

_____
_____
_____
_____
_____

Gratitude Entry #155

Acknowledging the good that you already have in your life is the foundation for all abundance.
—Eckhart Tolle

I'm grateful for_____

Affirmation of the day:
_____

How are you going to make yourself wait today?

_____
_____
_____
_____
_____

Gratitude Entry #156

There is as much greatness of mind in acknowledging a good turn, as in doing it.
—Seneca

I'm grateful for_____

Affirmation of the day:
_____

What are you going to do today that is outside of your comfort zone?

_____
_____
_____
_____
_____
_____

Gratitude Entry #157

As you keep your mind and heart focused in the right direction, approaching each day with faith and gratitude, I believe you will be empowered to live life to the fullest and enjoy the abundant life He has promised you!
—Victoria Osteen

I'm grateful for _____

Affirmation of the day:
_____

What is one SMART goal you have? (Specific. Measurable. Attainable. Relevant. Timely.)

_____
_____
_____
_____
_____
_____
_____
_____
_____
_____
_____
_____
_____
_____
_____
_____
_____
_____
_____

GRATITUDE ENTRY #158

Instead of being impatient because you have to wait for something be grateful for the extra time you have now to notice and appreciate your surroundings.
—Danielle Tinning

I'M GRATEFUL FOR_____

AFFIRMATION OF THE DAY:
_____

What are your triggers when you lose your patience? How are you grateful you figured them out so you can deal with them in a more positive manner?

_____
_____
_____
_____
_____
_____
_____
_____
_____
_____
_____
_____
_____
_____
_____
_____
_____
_____
_____
_____

Gratitude Entry #159

Gratitude can transform common days into thanksgivings, turn routine jobs into joy, and change ordinary opportunities into blessings.
—William Arthur Ward

I'm grateful for _____

Affirmation of the day:
_____

Write about a time you just had to laugh because of your impatience.
_____
_____
_____
_____
_____
_____

Gratitude Entry #160

The kind of experience of humility and happiness that comes with gratitude tends to crowd out whatever is coarse, or ugly, or mean.
—Kevin DeYoung

I'm grateful for _____

Affirmation of the day:
_____

What are amazing ways to relieve frustration so you aren't anxious?
_____
_____
_____
_____
_____
_____

Gratitude Entry #161

Gratitude will shift you to a higher frequency, and you will attract much better things.
—Rhonda Byrne

I'm grateful for _____

Affirmation of the day:
_____

When is a time you thought before you spoke and it saved you?

_____
_____
_____
_____
_____

Gratitude Entry #162

Gratitude is the sweetest thing in a seekers life — in all human life. If there is gratitude in your heart, then there will be tremendous sweetness in your eyes.
—Sri Chinmoy

I'm grateful for _____

Affirmation of the day:
_____

How do you trust that everything will work out in the end? How are you grateful that you can do this?

_____
_____
_____
_____
_____

Gratitude Entry #163

Thankfulness is the beginning of gratitude. Gratitude is the completion of thankfulness. Thankfulness may consist merely of words. Gratitude is shown in acts.
—Henri Frederic Amiel

I'M GRATEFUL FOR_____

AFFIRMATION OF THE DAY:
_____

Who is the most patient person you know and can emulate?

_____
_____
_____
_____
_____
_____
_____
_____
_____
_____
_____
_____
_____
_____
_____
_____
_____
_____
_____
_____

Gratitude Entry #164

Do not spoil what you have by desiring what you have not.
—Epicurus

I'm grateful for _____

Affirmation of the day:

_____

What is an uncontrollable event that happened to you and how did you embrace it in a positive patient way?

_____
_____
_____
_____
_____
_____
_____
_____
_____
_____
_____
_____
_____
_____
_____
_____
_____
_____
_____
_____
_____
_____

Gratitude Entry #165

Whatever life throws at me I'll take it and be grateful for it as well.
—Tom Felton

I'm grateful for _____

Affirmation of the day:

_____

Write about a time you were grateful that you released all your expectations?

_____
_____
_____
_____
_____
_____

Gratitude Entry #166

Being thankful is not always experienced as a natural state of existence, we must work at it, akin to a type of strength training for the heart.
—Larissa Gomez

I'm grateful for _____

Affirmation of the day:

_____

List five blessings you have received because of patience.

_____
_____
_____
_____
_____

Gratitude Entry #167

Appreciation is the purest vibration that exists on the planet today.
—Abraham Hicks

I'M GRATEFUL FOR _____

AFFIRMATION OF THE DAY:

_____

What does being on time mean to you? How has that increased your intimacy?

_____
_____
_____
_____
_____

Gratitude Entry #168

When I pray, I always thank Mother Nature for all the beauty in the world. It's about having an attitude of gratitude.
—Miranda Kerr

I'M GRATEFUL FOR _____

AFFIRMATION OF THE DAY:

_____

What is one thing you did today that required patience?

_____
_____
_____
_____
_____
_____

Gratitude Entry #169

There is only one thing that can form a bond between men, and that is gratitude…we cannot give someone else greater power over us than we have ourselves.
—Montesquieu

I'm grateful for _____

Affirmation of the day:
_____

How are you taking time to enjoy the process of life?

_____
_____
_____
_____
_____
_____
_____
_____
_____
_____
_____
_____
_____
_____
_____
_____
_____
_____
_____
_____
_____
_____
_____

Gratitude Entry #170

A grateful mind is a great mind which eventually attracts to itself great things.
—Plato

I'm grateful for _____

Affirmation of the day:
_____

Write about a time where you made a true connection.

Gratitude Entry #171

Develop an attitude of gratitude, and give thanks for everything that happens to you, knowing that every step forward is a step toward achieving something bigger and better than your current situation.
—Brian Tracy

I'M GRATEFUL FOR_____

AFFIRMATION OF THE DAY:
_____

How has your life flowed more fluidly since you've embraced patience?

Law of Attention

Gratitude Entry #172

Gratefulness is a double-edged sword. Because I think we've poured it into a feeling. And the batter of gratitude gets kind of stuck to the edges of the Williams Sonoma melamine mixing bowl. But gratefulness, the act of being grateful is actually…a verb. It's an activity.
—Abigail Spencer

I'm grateful for_____

Affirmation of the day:
_____

What kind of life experiences do you want to attract?

_____
_____
_____
_____
_____
_____
_____
_____
_____
_____
_____
_____
_____
_____
_____
_____
_____
_____
_____
_____
_____
_____
_____
_____

Gratitude Entry #173

Wear gratitude like a cloak and it will feed every corner of your life.
—Rumi

I'M GRATEFUL FOR _____

AFFIRMATION OF THE DAY:
_____

What exercises do you do to change your negative emotions in an instant?

_____
_____
_____
_____
_____
_____
_____
_____
_____
_____
_____
_____
_____
_____
_____
_____
_____
_____
_____
_____
_____
_____

Gratitude Entry #174

Let us rise up and be thankful, for if we didn't learn a lot today, at least we learned a little, and if we didn't learn a little, at least we didn't get sick, and if we got sick, at least we didn't die; so, let us all be thankful.
—Buddha

I'm grateful for _____

Affirmation of the day:
_____

List three positive changes you practiced today.

_____
_____
_____
_____
_____
_____

Gratitude Entry #175

Today I choose to live with gratitude for the love that fills my heart, the peace that rests within my spirit, and the voice of hope that says all things are possible.
—Anonymous

I'm grateful for _____

Affirmation of the day:
_____

List three fears and how you are going to conquer them.

_____
_____
_____
_____
_____
_____

Gratitude Entry #176

Appreciation can make a day, even change a life. Your willingness to put it into words is all that is necessary.
—Margaret Cousins

I'm grateful for _____

Affirmation of the day:
_____

List a fairly large goal you will hit by the end of the year.

_____
_____
_____
_____
_____
_____

Gratitude Entry #177

The longer you linger in gratitude, the more you draw your new life to you. For gratitude is the ultimate state of receivership.
—Dr. Joe Dispenza

I'm grateful for _____

Affirmation of the day:
_____

How were you grateful when you hit a milestone in your career?

_____
_____
_____
_____
_____
_____

Gratitude Entry #178

The Lord compensates the faithful for every loss. That which is taken away from those who love the Lord will be added unto them in his own way. While it may not come at the time we desire, the faithful will know that every tear today will eventually be returned a hundredfold with tears of rejoicing and gratitude.
—Joseph B. Wirthlin

I'm grateful for _____

Affirmation of the day:
_____

How have you become a more loving being?

_____
_____
_____
_____
_____
_____
_____
_____
_____
_____
_____
_____
_____
_____
_____
_____
_____
_____
_____
_____
_____

Gratitude Entry #179

In the New Testament, religion is grace and ethics is gratitude.
—Thomas Erskine

I'M GRATEFUL FOR _____

AFFIRMATION OF THE DAY:
_____

What experiences would you be grateful to have?

_____
_____
_____
_____
_____
_____
_____
_____
_____
_____
_____
_____
_____
_____
_____
_____
_____
_____
_____
_____

Gratitude Entry #180

Gratitude is a statement of certainty.
—David Cameron Gikandi

I'm grateful for_____

Affirmation of the day:
_____

What are you attracting right now?

_____
_____
_____
_____
_____
_____

Gratitude Entry #181

The hardest arithmetic to master is that which enables us to count our blessings.
—Eric Hoffer

I'm grateful for_____

Affirmation of the day:
_____

How are your thoughts and love creating an irresistible force for manifestation?

_____
_____
_____
_____
_____
_____

Gratitude Entry #182

Hardship is a blessing when it spurs effort and development; ease is a curse when it increases complacency and self-indulgence.
—Muso Kokushi

I'M GRATEFUL FOR_____

AFFIRMATION OF THE DAY:
_____

What brought you joy today?

_____
_____
_____
_____
_____
_____

Gratitude Entry #183

The most fortunate are those who have a wonderful capacity to appreciate again and again, freshly and naively, the basic goods of life, with awe, pleasure, wonder, and even ecstasy.
—Abraham Maslow

I'M GRATEFUL FOR_____

AFFIRMATION OF THE DAY:
_____

What small action did you take today to achieve your goal?

_____
_____
_____
_____
_____
_____

Gratitude Entry #184

No matter what's happening, choose to be happy. Don't focus on what's wrong. Find something positive in your life. Thank God for the small things.
—Joel Osteen

I'M GRATEFUL FOR _____

AFFIRMATION OF THE DAY:
_____

Write a thank you list to anything and/or anyone you feel you have forgotten to thank in the past.

GRATITUDE ENTRY #185

Showing gratitude is one of the simplest yet most powerful things humans can do for each other.
—Randy Pausch

I'M GRATEFUL FOR _____

AFFIRMATION OF THE DAY:
_____

Write about someone who inspires you.

Gratitude Entry #186

An early-morning walk is a blessing for the whole day.
—Henry David Thoreau

I'm grateful for_____

Affirmation of the day:
_____

I'm so happy and grateful now that...

_____
_____
_____
_____
_____
_____

Gratitude Entry #187

Gratefulness is the key to a happy life that we hold in our hands, because if we are not grateful, then no matter how much we have we will not be happy- because we will always want to have something else or something more.
—Brother David Steindl-Rast

I'm grateful for_____

Affirmation of the day:
_____

List five hobbies and activities that bring you joy.

_____
_____
_____
_____
_____
_____

Gratitude Entry #188

Be thankful for what you have; you'll end up having more. If you concentrate on what you don't have, you will never, ever have enough.
—Oprah Winfrey

I'm grateful for _____

Affirmation of the day:
_____

What aspects of your job do you enjoy the most?

_____
_____
_____
_____
_____
_____

Gratitude Entry #189

Love your mistake as much as your accomplishments. Because without mistakes, there wouldn't be any accomplishments.
—Anonymous

I'm grateful for _____

Affirmation of the day:
_____

List five things you like about your job or workplace.

_____
_____
_____
_____
_____
_____

Gratitude Entry #190

What can you do right now to turn your life around? Gratitude.
—Rhonda Byrne

I'M GRATEFUL FOR _____

AFFIRMATION OF THE DAY:
_____

Let your imagination run wild. Write about anything that comes to your mind first.

_____
_____
_____
_____
_____
_____
_____
_____
_____
_____
_____
_____
_____
_____
_____
_____
_____
_____
_____
_____

GRATITUDE ENTRY #191

When eating bamboo sprouts, remember the man who planted them.
—Chinese Proverb

I'M GRATEFUL FOR_____

AFFIRMATION OF THE DAY:
_____

Think about the qualities of the people you admire. List these qualities and how you can incorporate them in your life.

_____
_____
_____
_____
_____
_____
_____
_____
_____
_____
_____
_____
_____
_____
_____
_____
_____
_____
_____
_____
_____
_____

Gratitude Entry #192

He is a wise man who does not grieve for the things which he has not, but rejoices for those which he has.
—Epictetus

I'M GRATEFUL FOR _____

AFFIRMATION OF THE DAY:
_____

What is the best story you have ever heard about manifestation?

Law of Intention

Gratitude Entry #193

Gratitude is the inward feeling of kindness received. Thankfulness is the natural impulse to express that feeling. Thanksgiving is the following of that impulse.
—Henry Van Dyke

I'm grateful for _____

Affirmation of the day:

_____

How can you make your intention more loving?

Gratitude Entry #194

Gratitude is one of the least articulate of the emotions, especially when it is deep.
—Felix Frankfurter

I'm grateful for _____

Affirmation of the day:
_____

When have you felt you were in complete awareness?

_____
_____
_____
_____
_____
_____
_____

Gratitude Entry #195

When you truly acknowledge truly is yours. Invite your heart to be grateful and your 'thank you's' will be heard even when you don't use words.
—Pavithra Mehta

I'm grateful for _____

Affirmation of the day:
_____

What has been your favorite spiritual lesson to learn?

_____
_____
_____
_____
_____
_____
_____

Gratitude Entry #196

Have gratitude for the things you're discarding. By giving gratitude, you're giving closure to the relationship with that object, and by doing so, it becomes a lot easier to let go.
—Marie Kondo

I'm grateful for _____

Affirmation of the day:
_____

Replay your most recent negative event and visualize to a positive outcome.

_____
_____
_____
_____
_____
_____

Gratitude Entry #197

The real gift of gratitude is that the more grateful you are, the more present you become.
—Robert Holden

I'm grateful for _____

Affirmation of the day:
_____

What is a random act of kindness you did recently?

_____
_____
_____
_____
_____

Gratitude Entry #198

Let me encourage you to get up every day and focus on what you do have in life. Be thankful for the blessings of the little things, even when you don't get what you expect.
—Victoria Osteen

I'M GRATEFUL FOR_____

AFFIRMATION OF THE DAY:
_____

Write about a time where money was no object.

Gratitude Entry #199

Laughter is God's blessing.
—Joseph Prince

I'm grateful for _____

Affirmation of the day:

_____

What is on your vision board?

Gratitude Entry #200

A great many men's gratitude is nothing but a secret desire to hook in more valuable kindnesses hereafter.
—Francois de La Rochefoucauld

I'm grateful for_____

Affirmation of the day:
_____

What is a small win you accomplished in the past 24 hours?

_____
_____
_____
_____
_____
_____
_____

Gratitude Entry #201

For me, every hour is grace. And I feel gratitude in my heart each time I can meet someone and look at his or her smile.
—Elie Wiesel

I'm grateful for_____

Affirmation of the day:
_____

What are you most looking forward to this week?

_____
_____
_____
_____
_____
_____
_____

Gratitude Entry #202

Humor is mankind's greatest blessing.
—Mark Twain

I'm grateful for_____

Affirmation of the day:
_____

What have you done lately to strengthen your relationships?
_____
_____
_____
_____
_____
_____

Gratitude Entry #203

I'm a guy who has problems with moderation. All or nothing. Binge and purge. Kill or be killed. Gray is not a color I wear well. I should be dead. I know that. I should not be successful. I know that too. My daily existence is a toss of the coin – one side, fear, the other side, gratitude.
—Kurt Sutter

I'm grateful for_____

Affirmation of the day:
_____

What is your favorite possession?
_____
_____
_____
_____
_____
_____

Gratitude Entry #204

Wisdom and compassion should become the dominating influences that guide our thoughts, our words, and our actions.
—Anonymous

I'm grateful for _____

Affirmation of the day:
_____

I'm so grateful to have…

Gratitude Entry #205

I think gratitude is a big thing. It puts you in a place where you're humble.
—Andra Day

I'm grateful for _____

Affirmation of the day:

_____

What type of relationships are you grateful for?

_____
_____
_____
_____
_____
_____
_____
_____
_____
_____
_____
_____
_____
_____
_____
_____
_____
_____
_____
_____

Gratitude Entry #206

Gratitude is not only the greatest of virtues but the parent of all others.
—Marcus Tullius Cicero

I'm grateful for _____

Affirmation of the day:

_____

One thing I am really looking forward to is…

_____
_____
_____
_____
_____
_____

Gratitude Entry #207

Gratitude practice is really, really important to me. I think it's an incredible way to start your day.
—Rachel Hollis

I'm grateful for _____

Affirmation of the day:

_____

What inspires you to keep going when it's tough?

_____
_____
_____
_____
_____
_____

Gratitude Entry #208

It is one of the blessings of old friends that you can afford to be stupid with them.
—Ralph Waldo Emerson

I'm grateful for_____

Affirmation of the day:
_____

What do you love most about life?

_____
_____
_____
_____
_____
_____
_____
_____

Gratitude Entry #209

I have a lot of deficiencies, but gratitude is not one of them.
—Marshall Goldsmith

I'm grateful for_____

Affirmation of the day:
_____

What was the greatest gift you got that was free?

_____
_____
_____
_____
_____
_____
_____

Gratitude Entry #210

No one ever said learning was to be easy, but it's part of the process of evolving as a human being, and we all have to go through it. When I look back, I see that each difficult time brought an important lesson. And I prefer to look at it with gratitude because I wouldn't be who I am today if I haven't gone through it.
—Gisele Bündchen

I'M GRATEFUL FOR

AFFIRMATION OF THE DAY:

Where is a place you like to visit and why? What makes you want to go there?

Gratitude Entry #211

If you concentrate on finding whatever is good in every situation, you will discover that your life will suddenly be filled with gratitude, a feeling that nurtures the soul.
—Rabbi Harold Kushner

I'M GRATEFUL FOR _____

AFFIRMATION OF THE DAY:
_____

Write about a happy memory.

_____
_____
_____
_____
_____
_____
_____
_____
_____
_____
_____
_____
_____
_____
_____
_____
_____
_____
_____
_____
_____
_____
_____

Gratitude Entry #212

The moment one gives close attention to anything, even a blade of grass, it becomes a mysterious, awesome, indescribably magnificent world in itself.
—Henry Miller

I'M GRATEFUL FOR _____

AFFIRMATION OF THE DAY:

_____

What is one simple thing you can do to put yourself in a positive mood today?

_____
_____
_____
_____
_____
_____

Gratitude Entry #213

Gratitude is the ability to experience life as a gift. It liberates us from the prison of self-preoccupation.
—John Ortberg

I'M GRATEFUL FOR _____

AFFIRMATION OF THE DAY:

_____

Describe a small, everyday thing you enjoy.

_____
_____
_____
_____
_____
_____

Law of Abundance and Prosperity

Gratitude Entry #214

You don't get blessed, and feel blessed. You have to first feel blessed, then the blessings come to you.
—Roman Price

I'm grateful for _____

Affirmation of the day:

_____

Make an abundance list.

Gratitude Entry #215

Gratitude also opens your eyes to the limitless potential of the universe, while dissatisfaction closes your eyes to it.
—Stephen Richards

I'm grateful for _____

Affirmation of the day:
_____

What do you really appreciate about your life?
_____
_____
_____
_____
_____
_____

Gratitude Entry #216

I was in a space of gratitude. I'm so grateful to God for blessing me with an amazing family and the opportunity to do what I love.
—Jurnee Bell

I'm grateful for _____

Affirmation of the day:
_____

What is the biggest accomplishment in your personal life?
_____
_____
_____
_____
_____
_____
_____

Gratitude Entry #217

Gratitude for the present moment and the fullness of life now is the true prosperity.
—Eckhart Tolle

I'm grateful for _____

Affirmation of the day:
_____

What is the biggest accomplishment in your professional life?

_____
_____
_____
_____
_____
_____

Gratitude Entry #218

What seems to us as bitter trials are often blessings in disguise.
—Oscar Wilde

I'm grateful for _____

Affirmation of the day:
_____

How is your life more positive today than it was a year ago?

_____
_____
_____
_____
_____
_____

Gratitude Entry #219

If you want to turn your life around, try thankfulness. It will change your life mightily.
—Gerald Good

I'm grateful for _____

Affirmation of the day:
_____

Tell a story about when you praised someone in their field for their amazing accomplishments and meant it.

GRATITUDE ENTRY #220

In ordinary life, we hardly realize that we receive a great deal more than we give, and that it is only with gratitude that life becomes rich.
—Dietrich Bonhoeffer

I'M GRATEFUL FOR_____

AFFIRMATION OF THE DAY:
_____

Write about why you are worthy of wealth.

Gratitude Entry #221

If a fellow isn't thankful for what he's got, he isn't likely to be thankful for what he's going to get.
—Frank A. Clark

I'm grateful for _____

Affirmation of the day:

_____

What is a way you have made everyone prosper instead of feeling in competition with you?

_____
_____
_____
_____
_____
_____

Gratitude Entry #222

Gratitude is riches. Complaint is poverty.
—Doris Day

I'm grateful for _____

Affirmation of the day:

_____

One of my most worthwhile purchases has been my _____ How did it make you feel?

_____
_____
_____
_____
_____
_____

Gratitude Entry #223

I want to say thank you to all the people who walked into my life and made it outstanding, and all the people who walked out of my life and made it fantastic.
—Anonymous

I'm grateful for _____

Affirmation of the day:
_____

When did you last feel pure excitement?

_____
_____
_____
_____
_____
_____

Gratitude Entry #224

We must find time to stop and thank the people who make a difference in our lives.
—John F. Kennedy

I'm grateful for _____

Affirmation of the day:
_____

What is your ultimate favorite memory?

_____
_____
_____
_____
_____
_____

GRATITUDE ENTRY #225

Not what we say about our blessings, but how we use them, is the true measure of our thanksgiving.
—W.T. Purkiser

I'M GRATEFUL FOR_____

AFFIRMATION OF THE DAY:
_____

What were your three best days? Write a small paragraph about each day.

Gratitude Entry #226

Choosing to be positive and having a grateful attitude is going to determine how you're going to live your life.
—Joel Osteen

I'm grateful for _____

Affirmation of the day:
_____

What is the most beautiful place you have been to? Relive being in this place now. Describe it. How did it make you happy?

_____
_____
_____
_____
_____
_____
_____
_____
_____
_____
_____
_____
_____
_____
_____
_____
_____
_____
_____
_____

Gratitude Entry #227

If God miraculously created all that is, including you and me, then to say that we need miracles is an understatement. Our only response to that idea should be undying gratitude.
—Eric Metaxas

I'm grateful for _____

Affirmation of the day:
_____

What would you do if you had no fear?
_____
_____
_____
_____
_____
_____

Gratitude Entry #228

The soul that gives thanks can find comfort in everything; the soul that complains can find comfort in nothing.
—Hannah Whitall Smith

I'm grateful for _____

Affirmation of the day:
_____

What do you need to focus on to stay in an abundant mindset?
_____
_____
_____
_____
_____
_____

Gratitude Entry #229

I feel privileged with what I have…There's so much gratitude.
—Sophie Gregoire Trudeau

I'm grateful for _____

Affirmation of the day:
_____

Describe a time you wanted to say no but said yes, and it was completely worth it?

_____
_____
_____
_____
_____
_____

Gratitude Entry #230

Breathe. Let go. And remind yourself that this very moment is the only one you know you have for sure.
—Oprah Winfrey

I'm grateful for _____

Affirmation of the day:
_____

What's the best way to stop worrying and live in true abundance?

_____
_____
_____
_____
_____
_____

GRATITUDE ENTRY #231

I may not be where I want to be but I'm thankful for not being where I used to be.
—Habeeb Akande

I'M GRATEFUL FOR_____

AFFIRMATION OF THE DAY:
_____

Tell a story about how you rose from the ashes.

Gratitude Entry #232

I am full of gratitude for my life – and for this house.
—Julian Clary

I'm grateful for_____

Affirmation of the day:

_____

What is the hardest thing you've had to do, which led to a major personal accomplishment?

Gratitude Entry #233

Gratitude turns what we have into enough, and more. It turns denial into acceptance, chaos into order, confusion into clarity… it makes sense of our past, brings peace for today, and creates a vision for tomorrow.
—Melody Beattie

I'm grateful for _____

Affirmation of the day:
_____

List five things you have now that you didn't have five years ago.

_____
_____
_____
_____
_____

Gratitude Entry #234

Gratitude goes a long way.
—Sylvia Day

I'm grateful for _____

Affirmation of the day:
_____

List five major life accomplishments that you're proud to have achieved.

_____
_____
_____
_____
_____

GRATITUDE ENTRY #235

Live a life full of humility, gratitude, intellectual curiosity, and never stop learning.
—Gza

I'M GRATEFUL FOR_____

AFFIRMATION OF THE DAY:
_____

Look around the room and list all the items that you're grateful for.

_____
_____
_____
_____
_____
_____
_____
_____
_____
_____
_____
_____
_____
_____
_____
_____
_____
_____
_____
_____

Law of Karma

Gratitude Entry #236

I promise not to let you down. I will be your servant with all humility and gratitude.
—Mwai Kibaki

I'm grateful for_____

Affirmation of the day:

_____

Write about an amazing coincidence that wasn't such a coincidence at all.

_____
_____
_____
_____
_____
_____
_____

Gratitude Entry #237

When you view your world with an attitude of gratitude, you are training yourself to focus on the good in life.
—Paul J. Meyer

I'm grateful for_____

Affirmation of the day:

_____

Flip two complaints you have into positive fixes.

_____
_____
_____
_____
_____
_____
_____

Gratitude Entry #238

We often take for granted the very things that most deserve our gratitude.
—Cynthia Ozick

I'm grateful for _____

Affirmation of the day:

_____

Write a time when someone treated you poorly and how you reacted in a positive manner.

_____
_____
_____
_____
_____
_____

Gratitude Entry #239

Conversion is an offering of self, of love, and of loyalty we give to God in gratitude for the gift of testimony.
—David A Bednar

I'm grateful for _____

Affirmation of the day:

_____

How have you changed your karma for the better?

_____
_____
_____
_____
_____
_____

Gratitude Entry #240

If you don't embrace the bad, you can never truly embrace the good and be grateful and have gratitude for the tiniest things.
—Slowthai

I'm grateful for _____

Affirmation of the day:
_____

Who inspires you?

_____
_____
_____
_____
_____
_____
_____
_____
_____
_____
_____
_____
_____
_____
_____
_____
_____
_____
_____
_____
_____

Gratitude Entry #241

Feeling gratitude and not expressing it is like wrapping a present and not giving it.
—William Arthur Ward

I'm grateful for _____

Affirmation of the day:
_____

Write about a time when you volunteered.

_____
_____
_____
_____
_____
_____
_____
_____
_____
_____
_____
_____
_____
_____
_____
_____
_____
_____
_____
_____
_____
_____

Gratitude Entry #242

No duty is more urgent than that of returning thanks.
—James Allen

I'm grateful for_____

Affirmation of the day:
_____

What is your favorite charity and why do you support it?

_____
_____
_____
_____
_____
_____

Gratitude Entry #243

Make choices that bring love and joy to your body. It's not about perfection; it's about love and gratitude for an amazing body that works hard and deserves your respect.
—Alysia Reiner

I'm grateful for_____

Affirmation of the day:
_____

One generous thing I did recently was. . .

_____
_____
_____
_____
_____
_____
_____

Gratitude Entry #244

Gratitude is what you feel when you want what you already have.
—James Clear

I'm grateful for_____

Affirmation of the day:

_____

How are you able to help others?

_____
_____
_____
_____
_____
_____
_____

Gratitude Entry #245

I'm too grateful to be hateful. I am too blessed to be stressed.
—El DeBarge

I'm grateful for_____

Affirmation of the day:

_____

How have you made nature more beautiful?

_____
_____
_____
_____
_____
_____
_____

Gratitude Entry #246

Happiness is itself a kind of gratitude.
—Joseph Wood Krutch

I'm grateful for _____

Affirmation of the day:
_____

Express your gratitude today by thanking everyone who cares about you.

GRATITUDE ENTRY #247

As long as I am working, I am grateful and happy.
—Miriam Margolyes

I'M GRATEFUL FOR _____

AFFIRMATION OF THE DAY:
_____

Write about a time when you talked to an older generation and gained a new perspective.

Gratitude Entry #248

I am very grateful to God everyday that my eyes flutter open and I can jump out of the bed.
—Jerry Reed

I'm grateful for _____

Affirmation of the day:
_____

If you've been stuck in a routine, how did you change it?

_____
_____
_____
_____
_____
_____

Gratitude Entry #249

Look at everything as though you were seeing it for the first or the last time, then your time on earth will be filled with glory.
—Betty Smith

I'm grateful for _____

Affirmation of the day:
_____

What is something nice another person did for you today or this week?

_____
_____
_____
_____
_____
_____

Gratitude Entry #250

We can only be said to be alive in those moments when our hearts are conscious of our treasures.
—Thornton Wilder

I'm grateful for _____

Affirmation of the day:

_____

Write about a time someone went out of their way to help you.

_____
_____
_____
_____
_____
_____
_____

Gratitude Entry #251

Dwell on the beauty of life. Watch the stars, and see yourself running with them.
—Marcus Aurelius

I'm grateful for _____

Affirmation of the day:

_____

Write about a time you went out of your way to help someone.

_____
_____
_____
_____
_____
_____
_____

GRATITUDE ENTRY #252

The unthankful heart discovers no mercies; but the thankful heart will find, in every hour, some heavenly blessings.
—Henry Ward Beecher

I'M GRATEFUL FOR_____

AFFIRMATION OF THE DAY:
_____

Write about a teacher or mentor who has made an impact on your life.

GRATITUDE ENTRY #253

Gratitude is a powerful catalyst for happiness. It's the spark that lights a fire of joy in your soul.
—Amy Collette

I'M GRATEFUL FOR_____

AFFIRMATION OF THE DAY:
_____

Write about when a stranger changed your life.

Gratitude Entry #254

I feel a very unusual sensation – if it is not indigestion, I think it must be gratitude.
—Benjamin Disraeli

I'm grateful for _____

Affirmation of the day:
_____

Write about a lie you told and had to come clean, but are grateful you did?

_____
_____
_____
_____
_____
_____

Gratitude Entry #255

Gratitude is the most exquisite form of courtesy.
—Jacques Maritain

I'm grateful for _____

Affirmation of the day:
_____

Write about a time when you gave someone a spontaneous compliment and made their day.

_____
_____
_____
_____
_____
_____

Gratitude Entry #256

When you are grateful, fear disappears and abundance appears.
—Tony Robbins

I'm grateful for _____

Affirmation of the day:

_____

What is one small deed you can do for someone today?

_____
_____
_____
_____
_____
_____

Gratitude Entry #257

We love to commiserate and troubleshoot and prepare for the worst, and gratitude yanks us out of that and reminds us of the ridiculous amount of infinite blessings that are around us at all times.
—Jen Sincero

I'm grateful for _____

Affirmation of the day:

_____

List five ways you can share your gratitude with other people in the next 24 hours.

_____
_____
_____
_____
_____
_____

Law of Responsibility

Gratitude Entry #258

I finally realized that being grateful to my body was key to giving more love to myself.
—Oprah Winfrey

I'm grateful for _____

Affirmation of the day:

_____

How do you maintain balance in your life?

_____
_____
_____
_____
_____
_____
_____

Gratitude Entry #259

I am happy because I'm grateful. I choose to be grateful. That gratitude allows me to be happy.
—Will Arnett

I'm grateful for _____

Affirmation of the day:

_____

What did you do today that you took responsibility for?

_____
_____
_____
_____
_____
_____
_____

Gratitude Entry #260

A man's indebtedness is not virtue; his repayment is. Virtue begins when he dedicates himself actively to the job of gratitude.
—Ruth Benedict

I'm grateful for_____

Affirmation of the day:
_____

What are the best choices you've made that have shaped your life?

_____
_____
_____
_____
_____
_____
_____
_____
_____
_____
_____
_____
_____
_____
_____
_____
_____
_____
_____
_____
_____

Gratitude Entry #261

What makes me happy is the appreciation of people around me.
—Nadia Comaneci

I'm grateful for _____

Affirmation of the day:
_____

Write about a time you took full responsibility for your actions.

Gratitude Entry #262

If you have lived, take thankfully the past.
—John Dryden

I'm grateful for _____

Affirmation of the day:
_____

Name three events that happened to you which strengthened your character and who you are today (positive or negative).

_____
_____
_____
_____
_____

Gratitude Entry #263

It is necessary, then, to cultivate the habit of being grateful for every good thing that comes to you, and to give thanks continuously. And because all things have contributed to your advancement, you should include all things in your gratitude.
—Wallace D. Wattles

I'm grateful for _____

Affirmation of the day:
_____

What is a major lesson you've learned from your job?

_____
_____
_____
_____
_____

Gratitude Entry #264

Everyone enjoys being acknowledged and appreciated. Sometimes even the simplest act of gratitude can change someone's entire day. Take the time to recognize and value the people around you and appreciate those who make a difference in your lives.
—Roy T. Bennett

I'm grateful for_____

Affirmation of the day:

_____

Write about a recent obstacle you faced and how you overcame it.

_____
_____
_____
_____
_____
_____

Gratitude Entry #265

There are always flowers for those who want to see them.
—Henri Matisse

I'm grateful for_____

Affirmation of the day:

_____

What is a mistake you have made, which ultimately led to a positive experience?

_____
_____
_____
_____
_____
_____

GRATITUDE ENTRY #266

Two kinds of gratitude: The sudden kind we feel for what we take; the larger kind we feel for what we give.
—Edwin Arlington Robinson

I'M GRATEFUL FOR _____

AFFIRMATION OF THE DAY:
_____

What were your worst three days? How did those days make you grow as a person? Write a small paragraph about each day and think how much better off you are now.

_____
_____
_____
_____
_____
_____
_____
_____
_____
_____
_____
_____
_____
_____
_____
_____
_____
_____
_____
_____
_____

Gratitude Entry #267

Gratitude is one of the most medicinal emotions we can feel. It elevates our moods and fills us with joy.
—Sara Avant Stover

I'M GRATEFUL FOR_____

AFFIRMATION OF THE DAY:
_____

List two struggles you experienced in life that you have overcome. What or who has helped you to defeat these trials?

_____
_____
_____
_____
_____
_____
_____
_____
_____
_____
_____
_____
_____
_____
_____
_____
_____
_____
_____
_____
_____
_____

Gratitude Entry #268

Forget injuries, never forget kindnesses.
—Confucius

I'm grateful for _____

Affirmation of the day:
_____

One of my greatest life lessons is. . .

_____
_____
_____
_____
_____
_____

Gratitude Entry #269

Gratitude is the memory of the heart.
—Jean-Baptiste Massieu

I'm grateful for _____

Affirmation of the day:
_____

One way I have bettered myself in the past month is. . .

_____
_____
_____
_____
_____
_____

Gratitude Entry #270

Stop thinking gratitude as a byproduct of your circumstances and start thinking of it as a world view.
—Bryan Robles

I'M GRATEFUL FOR_____

AFFIRMATION OF THE DAY:
_____

One thing that always makes me feel better when I'm down is. . .

_____
_____
_____
_____
_____
_____

Gratitude Entry #271

When I wake up in the morning, I like to express my gratitude for being on the planet. That gratefulness makes me very present.
—Trudie Styler

I'M GRATEFUL FOR_____

AFFIRMATION OF THE DAY:
_____

What mistake or failure are you grateful for?

_____
_____
_____
_____
_____
_____

GRATITUDE ENTRY #272

When we give cheerfully and accept gratefully, everyone is blessed.
—Maya Angelou

I'M GRATEFUL FOR _____

AFFIRMATION OF THE DAY:
_____

Describe a painful experience that made you a stronger person.

Gratitude Entry #273

Being thankful not only shows good manners, but a simple expression of thankfulness can go a long way in relationships and communication with others. It is not only enhances our own lives, but makes other people feel appreciated.
—Daniella Whyte

I'M GRATEFUL FOR_____

AFFIRMATION OF THE DAY:
_____

Write about a time you stopped feeling sorry for yourself and pushed through barriers.

Gratitude Entry #274

Learn to be thankful for what you already have, while you pursue all that you want.
—Jim Rohn

I'm grateful for_____

Affirmation of the day:
_____

What is one thing you're really proud of?

_____
_____
_____
_____
_____
_____
_____

Gratitude Entry #275

Social scientists have found that the fastest way to feel happiness is to practice gratitude.
—Chip Conley

I'm grateful for_____

Affirmation of the day:
_____

Write about a time you felt confident.

_____
_____
_____
_____
_____
_____

Gratitude Entry #276

We should certainly count our blessings, but we should also make our blessings count.
—Neal A. Maxwell

I'm grateful for _____

Affirmation of the day:
_____

How did you get out of your self-sabotaging behavior?

_____
_____
_____
_____
_____
_____

Gratitude Entry #277

On the recollection of so many and great favors and blessings, I now, with a high sense of gratitude, presume to offer up my sincere thanks to the Almighty, the Creator and Preserver.
—William Bartram

I'm grateful for _____

Affirmation of the day:
_____

Write about what values you have to offer the world.

_____
_____
_____
_____
_____
_____

Gratitude Entry #278

Fill the earth with your songs of gratitude.
—Charles Spurgeon

I'm grateful for _____

Affirmation of the day:
_____

Write about a time you failed, and it was perfectly okay that you did.

Gratitude Entry #279

No one who achieves success does so without the help of others. The wise and confident acknowledge this help with gratitude.
—Alfred North Whitehead

I'M GRATEFUL FOR_____

AFFIRMATION OF THE DAY:
_____

Write about a time when you finally realized you were good enough.

_____
_____
_____
_____
_____
_____
_____
_____
_____
_____
_____
_____
_____
_____
_____
_____
_____
_____
_____
_____
_____
_____
_____

Law of Forgiveness

Gratitude Entry #280

If you can't reward then you should thank.
—Arabic Proverb

I'm grateful for _____

Affirmation of the day:
_____

Write a letter forgiving yourself.

Gratitude Entry #281

Gratitude unlocks all that's blocking us from really feeling truthful, really feeling authentic and vulnerable and happy.
—Gabrielle Bernstein

I'M GRATEFUL FOR_____

AFFIRMATION OF THE DAY:
_____

How do you practice empathy?

_____
_____
_____
_____
_____
_____
_____

Gratitude Entry #282

There are some things I wish I never knew, but I am grateful for things that I have learned, too.
—A.J. Cook

I'M GRATEFUL FOR_____

AFFIRMATION OF THE DAY:
_____

How has suffering made you a better person?

_____
_____
_____
_____
_____
_____
_____

Gratitude Entry #283

Joy is a heart full and a mind purified by gratitude.
—Marietta McCarty

I'm grateful for _____

Affirmation of the day:

_____

When was a time you decided to choose happiness instead of being right?

_____
_____
_____
_____
_____
_____
_____

Gratitude Entry #284

Whatever you appreciate and give thanks for will increase in your life.
—Sanaya Roman

I'm grateful for _____

Affirmation of the day:

_____

How have you healed with grace?

_____
_____
_____
_____
_____
_____
_____

Gratitude Entry #285

...it is not joy that makes us grateful; it is gratitude that makes us joyful.
—David Steindl-Rast

I'm grateful for _____

Affirmation of the day:
_____

Write a letter forgiving your parents for any negative things they did that you might still be holding onto.

_____
_____
_____
_____
_____
_____
_____
_____
_____
_____
_____
_____
_____
_____
_____
_____
_____
_____
_____
_____
_____
_____

Gratitude Entry #286

It's not possible to experience constant euphoria, but if you're grateful, you can find happiness in everything.
—Pharrell Williams

I'm grateful for _____

Affirmation of the day:
_____

Write a forgiveness letter to someone who hurt you.

Gratitude Entry #287

Be grateful for what you already have while you pursue your goals. If you aren't grateful for what you already have, what makes you think you would be happy with more.
—Roy T. Bennett

I'm grateful for _____

Affirmation of the day:
_____

Talk about a time when someone was putting someone down and you stood up for that person.

_____
_____
_____
_____
_____
_____

Gratitude Entry #288

Giving is an expression of gratitude for our blessings.
—Laura Arrillaga-Andreessen

I'm grateful for _____

Affirmation of the day:
_____

What burdens were released when you forgave someone?

_____
_____
_____
_____
_____
_____

Gratitude Entry #289

Three meals plus bedtime make four sure blessings a day.
—Mason Cooley

I'M GRATEFUL FOR_____

AFFIRMATION OF THE DAY:
_____

What was the ultimate gift you gave yourself once you forgave all your past hardships?

_____
_____
_____
_____
_____
_____

Gratitude Entry #290

My socks may not match, but my feet are always warm.
—Maureen McCullough

I'M GRATEFUL FOR_____

AFFIRMATION OF THE DAY:
_____

Is there something you resent right now that you need to forgive?

_____
_____
_____
_____
_____
_____

Gratitude Entry #291

I'm looking forward to the future, and feeling grateful for the past.
—Mike Rowe

I'm grateful for _____

Affirmation of the day:

_____

Write about forgiving all of your regrets.

GRATITUDE ENTRY #292

Silent gratitude isn't very much to anyone.
—Gertrude Stein

I'M GRATEFUL FOR_____

AFFIRMATION OF THE DAY:
_____

Write about forgiving all of your past judgments.

Gratitude Entry #293

Gratitude is a mark of a noble soul and a refined character. We like to be around those who are grateful.
—Joseph B. Wirthlin

I'm grateful for _____

Affirmation of the day:
_____

How do you practice mindfulness?

_____
_____
_____
_____
_____
_____

Gratitude Entry #294

When we focus on our gratitude, the tide of disappointment goes out and the tide of love rushes in.
—Kristin Armstrong

I'm grateful for _____

Affirmation of the day:
_____

When have you found meaning and strength through your pain?

_____
_____
_____
_____
_____
_____

Gratitude Entry #295

The unthankful heart discovers no mercies; but the thankful heart will find in every hour, some heavenly blessings.
—Henry Ward Beecher

I'M GRATEFUL FOR _____

AFFIRMATION OF THE DAY:
_____

What helps you release your pain that you're grateful for?

_____
_____
_____
_____
_____
_____
_____

Gratitude Entry #296

Every breath we draw is a gift of God's love; every moment of existence is a grace.
—Thomas Merton

I'M GRATEFUL FOR _____

AFFIRMATION OF THE DAY:
_____

What type of healing took place after you forgave people that hurt you?

_____
_____
_____
_____
_____
_____
_____

Gratitude Entry #297

Giving thanks for abundance is greater than the abundance itself.
—Rumi

I'm grateful for _____

Affirmation of the day:
_____

Write a letter releasing all the hate and anger from your heart.

Gratitude Entry #298

Train yourself never to put off the word or action for the expression of gratitude.
—Albert Schweitzer

I'm grateful for _____

Affirmation of the day:

_____

Flip your perspective and write about the other person who has hurt you. Write it through empathy.

Gratitude Entry #299

Sometimes we should express our gratitude for the small and simple things like the scent of the rain, the taste of your favorite food, or the sound of a loved one's voice.
—Joseph B. Wirthlin

I'm grateful for _____

Affirmation of the day:
_____

When you forgave, how did that shift your energy?

_____
_____
_____
_____
_____

Gratitude Entry #300

Believe that good things will happen and they will.
—Anonymous

I'm grateful for _____

Affirmation of the day:
_____

Who has forgiven you for a mistake you've made in the past? How have you made amends?

_____
_____
_____
_____
_____

Law of No Judgment

Gratitude Entry #301

Got no check books, got no banks. Still I'd like to express my thanks — I got the sun in the morning and the moon at night.
—Irving Berlin

I'm grateful for _____

Affirmation of the day:

_____

Write about a day in another person's shoes.

Gratitude Entry #302

There's no happier person than a truly thankful, content person.
—Joyce Meyer

I'm grateful for _____

Affirmation of the day:

_____

Write about something that happened with a new friend recently.

Gratitude Entry #303

He enjoys much who is thankful for little.
—Thomas Secker

I'm grateful for _____

Affirmation of the day:
_____

Write about a limited view you had, then when you did more research, it opened your eyes.

_____
_____
_____
_____
_____
_____

Gratitude Entry #304

Gratitude is one of those things that cannot be bought. It must be born with men, or else all the obligations in the world will not create it.
—Edward Wood

I'm grateful for _____

Affirmation of the day:
_____

Turn three judgements into positive perspectives.

_____
_____
_____
_____
_____

GRATITUDE ENTRY #305

Be grateful, not only for others, but for yourself.
—Anonymous

I'M GRATEFUL FOR _____

AFFIRMATION OF THE DAY:

_____

List three things you could do today to be a kinder person.

_____
_____
_____
_____
_____
_____

GRATITUDE ENTRY #306

Piglet noticed that even though he had a very small heart, it could hold a rather large amount of gratitude.
—A.A. Milne

I'M GRATEFUL FOR _____

AFFIRMATION OF THE DAY:

_____

Write about a good experience with customer service.

_____
_____
_____
_____
_____
_____

GRATITUDE ENTRY #307

We are constituted so that simple acts of kindness, such as giving to charity or expressing gratitude, have a positive effect on our long-term moods. The key to the happy life, it seems, is the good life: a life with sustained relationships, challenging work, and connections to community.
—Paul Bloom

I'M GRATEFUL FOR _____

AFFIRMATION OF THE DAY:
_____

Write a letter to someone you judged harshly and thank them for teaching you a lesson.

GRATITUDE ENTRY #308

Nothing is more honorable than a grateful heart.
—Seneca

I'M GRATEFUL FOR_____

AFFIRMATION OF THE DAY:
_____

If you have ever put yourself down, write an inspirational letter to yourself.

_____
_____
_____
_____
_____
_____
_____
_____
_____
_____
_____
_____
_____
_____
_____
_____
_____
_____
_____
_____

Gratitude Entry #309

Our prayers should be for blessings in general, for God knows best what is good for us.
—Socrates

I'M GRATEFUL FOR _____

AFFIRMATION OF THE DAY:
_____

When was a time you judged someone too quickly then found their story amazing?

_____
_____
_____
_____
_____
_____

Gratitude Entry #310

Be grateful for what you have, work hard for what you don't have.
—Anonymous

I'M GRATEFUL FOR _____

AFFIRMATION OF THE DAY:
_____

When was a time you finally accepted someone for who they are?

_____
_____
_____
_____
_____
_____

Gratitude Entry #311

I've had a remarkable life. I seem to be in such good places at the right time. You know, if you were to ask me to sum my life up in one word, gratitude.
—Dietrich Bonhoeffer

I'm grateful for _____

Affirmation of the day:
_____

What does compassion mean to you?

_____
_____
_____
_____
_____
_____

Gratitude Entry #312

Always remember to smile and look up at what you got in life.
—Marilyn Monroe

I'm grateful for _____

Affirmation of the day:
_____

Write about your favorite inspirational song that makes you want to be a better person.

_____
_____
_____
_____
_____
_____

Gratitude Entry #313

What I myself experience is indescribable gratitude in the face of God's perpetual and preemptive love, a love which is not contingent upon requital or even belief in His existence.
—Franz Wright

I'm grateful for_____

Affirmation of the day:
_____

Write about a story that melted your heart.

Gratitude Entry #314

Talent is God given. Be humble. Fame is man-given. Be grateful. Conceit is self-given. Be careful.
—John Wooden

I'M GRATEFUL FOR_____

AFFIRMATION OF THE DAY:
_____

Write a letter to your inner child.

Gratitude Entry #315

Let us live simply in the freshness of the present moment, in the clarity of pure awakened mind.
—Anonymous

I'm grateful for_____

Affirmation of the day:
_____

What book changed your outlook on life?

_____
_____
_____
_____
_____
_____

Gratitude Entry #316

One can never pay in gratitude; one can only pay 'in kind' somewhere else in life.
—Anne Morrow Lindbergh

I'm grateful for_____

Affirmation of the day:
_____

Write about a time you wanted to say something negative and flipped the switch instantly.

_____
_____
_____
_____
_____
_____

Gratitude Entry #317

One of the surest evidences of friendship that one individual can display to another is telling him gently of a fault. If any other can excel it, it is listening to such a disclosure with gratitude, and amending the error.
—Edward G. Bulwer-Lytton

I'm grateful for _____

Affirmation of the day:
_____

When was a time you stood up for yourself?

_____
_____
_____
_____
_____
_____

Gratitude Entry #318

Gratitude to gratitude always gives birth.
—Sophocles

I'm grateful for _____

Affirmation of the day:
_____

Write about how you have overcome jealousy.

_____
_____
_____
_____
_____
_____

Gratitude Entry #319

Things turn out best for people who make the best of the way things turn out.
—John Wooden

I'M GRATEFUL FOR_____

AFFIRMATION OF THE DAY:
_____

What difficulties have made you a stronger person?

_____
_____
_____
_____
_____
_____
_____
_____
_____
_____
_____
_____
_____
_____
_____
_____
_____
_____
_____
_____
_____

Gratitude Entry #320

While it may be difficult to change the world, it is always possible to change the way we look at it.
—Anonymous

I'm grateful for _____

Affirmation of the day:
_____

What hardships have almost defeated you, but you persevered?

Gratitude Entry #321

Joy is the simplest form of gratitude.
—Karl Barth

I'M GRATEFUL FOR _____

AFFIRMATION OF THE DAY:
_____

Write a loving poem.

Law of Unconditional Love and Gratitude

GRATITUDE ENTRY #322

Gratitude can turn a meal into a feast.
—Melody Beattie

I'M GRATEFUL FOR_____

AFFIRMATION OF THE DAY:
_____

Write a story about love.

Gratitude Entry #323

God gave us our relatives; thank God we can choose our friends.
—Ethel Watts Mumford

I'M GRATEFUL FOR_____

AFFIRMATION OF THE DAY:
_____

Who frustrates you? Write three positive things about them and why they are worthy of love.

_____
_____
_____
_____
_____
_____

Gratitude Entry #324

If you are really thankful, what do you do? You share.
—W. Clement Stone

I'M GRATEFUL FOR_____

AFFIRMATION OF THE DAY:
_____

What is your favorite message about love?

_____
_____
_____
_____
_____

Gratitude Entry #325

Yesterday is history. Tomorrow is a mystery. But today is a gift. That's why they call it the present.
—Anonymous

I'm grateful for _____

Affirmation of the day:
_____

Write about how you want to be shown love.

_____
_____
_____
_____
_____
_____

Gratitude Entry #326

Gratitude is the fairest blossom that springs from the soul.
—Henry Ward Beecher

I'm grateful for _____

Affirmation of the day:
_____

Write about a time you got butterflies in your stomach.

_____
_____
_____
_____
_____
_____

Gratitude Entry #327

I have embraced every day with gratitude.
—Nadya Suleman

I'm grateful for _____

Affirmation of the day:
_____

Write a love letter to yourself.

Gratitude Entry #328

God gave you a gift of 84,600 seconds today. Have you used one of them to say thank you?
—William Arthur Ward

I'M GRATEFUL FOR _____

AFFIRMATION OF THE DAY:
_____

Write "I love myself" until you believe it.

Gratitude Entry #329

The thing I'm most grateful for right now is elastic waistbands.
—Anonymous

I'M GRATEFUL FOR _____

AFFIRMATION OF THE DAY:

_____

Describe a family tradition you are most grateful for.

_____
_____
_____
_____
_____
_____

Gratitude Entry #330

It's a sign of mediocrity when you demonstrate gratitude with moderation.
—Roberto Benigni

I'M GRATEFUL FOR _____

AFFIRMATION OF THE DAY:

_____

Write about someone who makes your life better.

_____
_____
_____
_____
_____
_____
_____

Gratitude Entry #331

We should honor Mother Earth with gratitude; otherwise our spirituality may become hypocritical.
—Radhanath Swami

I'm grateful for _____

Affirmation of the day:
_____

What was the last gift you enjoyed receiving?

_____
_____
_____
_____
_____
_____
_____

Gratitude Entry #332

There is always, always, always something to be thankful for.
—Anonymous

I'm grateful for _____

Affirmation of the day:
_____

What animals have positively impacted your life?

_____
_____
_____
_____
_____
_____
_____

GRATITUDE ENTRY #333

Be thankful for everything that happens in your life; it's all an experience.
—Roy T. Bennett

I'M GRATEFUL FOR_____

AFFIRMATION OF THE DAY:
_____

Write a love letter to mother nature.

Gratitude Entry #334

A person can almost be defined by his or her attitude toward gratitude.
—Elie Wiesel

I'm grateful for _____

Affirmation of the day:
_____

What family members are you most grateful for? Write about what makes them special.

_____
_____
_____
_____
_____
_____
_____
_____
_____
_____
_____
_____
_____
_____
_____
_____
_____
_____
_____
_____
_____
_____
_____
_____

Gratitude Entry #335

Sometimes we need to remind ourselves that thankfulness is indeed a virtue.
—William Bennett

I'm grateful for _____

Affirmation of the day:

_____

Write about something beautiful you saw today.

_____
_____
_____
_____
_____
_____

Gratitude Entry #336

The smallest thanks is always worth more than the effort it takes to give it.
—Anonymous

I'm grateful for _____

Affirmation of the day:

_____

What memory are you most grateful for?

_____
_____
_____
_____
_____
_____

Gratitude Entry #337

Nothing new can come into your life unless you are grateful for what you already have.
—Michael Bernard

I'm grateful for_____

Affirmation of the day:
_____

Write about a moment in your life that was filled with pure joy and unconditional love.

_____
_____
_____
_____
_____
_____

Gratitude Entry #338

The smallest act of kindness is worth than the grandest intention.
—Oscar Wilde

I'm grateful for_____

Affirmation of the day:
_____

Who has taught you about unconditional love in the past or present? And how did they show it?

_____
_____
_____
_____
_____
_____

GRATITUDE ENTRY #339

An attitude of gratitude brings great things.
—Yogi Bhajan

I'M GRATEFUL FOR_____

AFFIRMATION OF THE DAY:
_____

Write a love letter to someone who needs to hear from you.

Gratitude Entry #340

If you haven't all the things you want, be grateful for the things you don't have that you wouldn't want.
—Anonymous

I'M GRATEFUL FOR _____

AFFIRMATION OF THE DAY:
_____

Who was the last person you hugged? Describe it.

_____
_____
_____
_____
_____
_____
_____
_____
_____
_____
_____
_____
_____
_____
_____
_____
_____
_____
_____
_____

Gratitude Entry #341

The thankful receiver bears a plentiful harvest.
—William Blake

I'm grateful for _____

Affirmation of the day:
_____

How did it feel the first time you fell in love?

_____
_____
_____
_____
_____
_____
_____

Gratitude Entry #342

The highest tribute to the dead is not grief but gratitude.
—Thornton Wilder

I'm grateful for _____

Affirmation of the day:
_____

Who did you last say "I love you" to? Why do you love them? Describe.

_____
_____
_____
_____
_____
_____

Gratitude Entry #343

There is a calmness to a life lived in gratitude, a quiet joy.
—Ralph H. Blum

I'M GRATEFUL FOR_____

AFFIRMATION OF THE DAY:
_____

How do you express your love to others?

Law of Oneness

Gratitude Entry #344

If you can't be content with what you have received, be thankful for what you have escaped.
—Anonymous

I'm grateful for_____

Affirmation of the day:
_____

Write about a magical time you had déjà vu.

_____
_____
_____
_____
_____
_____

Gratitude Entry #345

Gratitude changes the pangs of memory into a tranquil joy.
—Dietrich Bonhoeffer

I'm grateful for_____

Affirmation of the day:
_____

How would you like to improve a stranger's day today?

_____
_____
_____
_____
_____
_____

Gratitude Entry #346

A moment of gratitude makes a difference in your attitude.
—Bruce Wilkinson

I'M GRATEFUL FOR _____

AFFIRMATION OF THE DAY:
_____

Write about a time you met someone and they instantly became your best friend.

Gratitude Entry #347

Focus on the positives and be grateful.
—Katrina Bowden

I'm grateful for_____

Affirmation of the day:
_____

Write about nature, whatever comes to mind.

Gratitude Entry #348

It is not happy people who are thankful, it is thankful people who are happy.
—Anonymous

I'M GRATEFUL FOR _____

AFFIRMATION OF THE DAY:
_____

If we were all one, what would you change immediately to help people see the light?

_____
_____
_____
_____
_____
_____

Gratitude Entry #349

Gratitude and attitude are not challenges; they are choices.
—Robert Braathe

I'M GRATEFUL FOR _____

AFFIRMATION OF THE DAY:
_____

Write about a time you had six degrees of separation with someone.

_____
_____
_____
_____
_____

Gratitude Entry #350

I believe gratitude leads to happiness.
—Nafessa Williams

I'm grateful for _____

Affirmation of the day:

_____

What type of people do you surround yourself with? Why?

_____
_____
_____
_____
_____
_____

Gratitude Entry #351

Enjoy the little things, for one day you may look back and realize they were the big things.
—Robert Brault

I'm grateful for _____

Affirmation of the day:

_____

How will you improve a family member's day this week?

_____
_____
_____
_____
_____
_____

Gratitude Entry #352

I am someone who is so grateful and practice gratitude every single day.
—Bishop Briggs

I'M GRATEFUL FOR_____

AFFIRMATION OF THE DAY:
_____

What do your faith and beliefs mean to you?

_____
_____
_____
_____
_____
_____
_____
_____
_____
_____
_____
_____
_____
_____
_____
_____
_____
_____
_____
_____
_____
_____

Gratitude Entry #353

It is impossible to feel grateful and depressed in the same moment.
—Naomi Williams

I'M GRATEFUL FOR _____

AFFIRMATION OF THE DAY:
_____

What friends are you most grateful for? List what makes each friend special.

_____
_____
_____
_____
_____
_____
_____
_____
_____
_____
_____
_____
_____
_____
_____
_____
_____
_____
_____
_____
_____
_____

Gratitude Entry #354

Feeling gratitude isn't born in us — it's something we are taught, and in turn, we teach our children.
— Joyce Brothers

I'm grateful for _____

Affirmation of the day:
_____

Write about something in your community that you are thankful for.

_____
_____
_____
_____
_____
_____

Gratitude Entry #355

I am filled with so much sincerity and gratitude to know where I came from and what I'm doing now.
—Antonio Brown

I'm grateful for _____

Affirmation of the day:
_____

One person I don't talk to very often, but I know I can count on is. . .

_____
_____
_____
_____
_____
_____

Gratitude Entry #356

Gratitude is an opener of locked-up blessings.
—Marianne Williamson

I'm grateful for _____

Affirmation of the day:
_____

I know I'm not alone in this life because...

_____
_____
_____
_____
_____
_____

Gratitude Entry #357

We're a nation hungry for more joy: because we're starving from a lack of gratitude.
—Brené Brown

I'm grateful for _____

Affirmation of the day:
_____

What wisdom has come with age?

_____
_____
_____
_____
_____
_____

Gratitude Entry #358

Gratitude is not only the memory but the homage of the heart rendered to God for his goodness.
—Nathaniel Parker Willis

I'm grateful for _____

Affirmation of the day:

_____

Describe your oldest friend. What do you like most about this person?

Gratitude Entry #359

Always have an attitude for gratitude.
—Sterling K. Brown

I'm grateful for _____

Affirmation of the day:

_____

Write about someone who made a positive difference in your life.

_____
_____
_____
_____
_____
_____
_____
_____
_____
_____
_____
_____
_____
_____
_____
_____
_____
_____
_____
_____
_____
_____
_____
_____

Gratitude Entry #360

True forgiveness is when you can say, "Thank you for that experience."
—Oprah Winfrey

I'M GRATEFUL FOR_____

AFFIRMATION OF THE DAY:
_____

Write about a time you took a nature walk and described what you observed.

_____
_____
_____
_____
_____
_____

Gratitude Entry #361

You have no cause for anything but gratitude and joy.
—Buddha

I'M GRATEFUL FOR_____

AFFIRMATION OF THE DAY:
_____

Write about something you saw recently that warmed your heart.

_____
_____
_____
_____
_____
_____

Gratitude Entry #362

Love and gratitude can part seas, move mountains, and create miracles.
—Rhonda Byrne

I'M GRATEFUL FOR _____

AFFIRMATION OF THE DAY:
_____

Describe a weird family tradition that you love.

_____
_____
_____
_____
_____
_____

Gratitude Entry #363

I live by two words: tenacity and gratitude.
—Henry Winkler

I'M GRATEFUL FOR _____

AFFIRMATION OF THE DAY:
_____

What is your favorite quote or a bit of wisdom that you frequently share with others?

_____
_____
_____
_____
_____

Gratitude Entry #364

You won't be happy with more until you're happy with what you've got.
—Viki King

I'M GRATEFUL FOR _____

AFFIRMATION OF THE DAY:

_____

What is your favorite holiday memory?

Gratitude Entry #365

Love those who appreciate you, and appreciate those who love you.
—Connor Chalfant

I'M GRATEFUL FOR_____

AFFIRMATION OF THE DAY:
_____

What makes you feel safe?

www.ingramcontent.com/pod-product-compliance
Lightning Source LLC
Chambersburg PA
CBHW081153070526
44583CB00021B/2812